SMART HOUSE-KEEPING

for
Modern Women

Published by
Lotus Press

SMART HOUSE-KEEPING
for
Modern Women

Nisha Bhasin

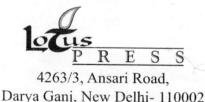
Lotus PRESS

4263/3, Ansari Road,
Darya Ganj, New Delhi- 110002

Lotus Press

4263/3, Ansari Road, Darya Ganj, New Delhi- 110002
Ph.: 32903912, 23280047, E-mail: lotus_press@sify.com
www.lotuspress.co.in

Smart House-Keeping for Modern Women
© 2010, Lotus Press
ISBN 978-81-8382-219-0

Published by: **Lotus Press**, New Delhi.
Printed at: DD Offset Printing Prees, Noida

PREFACE

A task more than just mopping and moving around with a broom, house keeping is that essential element which makes a home worth living.

From preparing meals for oneself and family, to cleaning and managing other domestic concerns, the simple looking task of house keeping can be actually a great struggle.

For the working men and women, it may be just cleaning and making the house presentable, while for a homemaker, the task stands as a compliment to her virtues.

While the way a house looks speaks about the people who live in it, at the same time it also reminds every person who lives in it the responsibilities he has towards maintaining it.

The present book on housekeeping gives a detailed account of the various things involved in making a house a better place to live in. From everyday and seasonal cleaning tips to improving interpersonal relationships and decorating the house in cost effective manner every aspect involved in the making of a happy home is covered explicitly and described through pictures and in easy to understand language.

The quick tips given the book are handy and easy to employ. They are meant to help a reader maintain his/her home in a cost effective manner, making it a presentable and comfortable place.

Indeed, everybody wants a home that he can boast of. The book shows how even smaller apartments can be maintained in a manner that they attract admirable attention of every visitor.

Hope the book would bring quality improvements in the readers life and help them make their home a pleasant heaven.

Author

CONTENTS

CHAPTER 1

Importance of House-Keeping

Every woman takes pride in boasting a beautiful home. Apart from the happiness she gets on seeing a well maintained home, it is also a goal for her, as often she is judged by the way she keeps her house. For her, it's like a temple — a key through which she can ensure the highest level of physical and emotional comfort for her family. And, in view of its critical significance in one's life, it's imperative that a home is managed well. It's an art every homemaker must master.

While we use the term house-keeping, we often associate it with cleaning up a place once a week. But, house-keeping is not such a limited term, as it is an important factor for safety, health, production and morale of any place. Moreover, house-keeping is a work which is not designated to only one person. It is everyone's duty to make the place he or she lives in neat, clean and free of obstructions. The general cleanliness of the house is important for the hygiene of the house, which in turn ensures the health of its members. Instead of thinking of house-keeping as some tedious and depressing job, follow a few time tested methods to make house-keeping seem not as a job but

11

as a healthy activity. This book will provide some helpful tips which would help in making home a healthier and a safer place to live in.

To start with the process of house-keeping, one must know the basic tasks involved in it. First and foremost, one needs to keep one's house clean to prevent it from attack of micro-organisms like fungi, bacteria and virus, which are prominent in kitchen and bathroom areas of the house. Instead of facing an uphill task after months of accumulated dust and germs, one should regularly clean the house to keep it hygienic and healthy. A good idea is to have hardwood floors in the house in colder areas, as they are easy to maintain and last for many years.

Other than cleanliness, house-keeping also involves saving the fun and memorable moments of life. This involves protecting family photos by digitising the prints so that memories do not fade with time. In addition, one also faces the problem of safely storing clothes. Always clean the garments before storing and ensure to safeguard them from termites by safely storing them with naphthalene balls. It is not only the woman's job to undertake entire house-keeping responsibilities on her. Instill these positive and healthy habits in children also, so that the entire family works together for healthy and safe living.

Focusing on other tasks of the house-keeping, one must then take care of the monetary budget of the home. It includes the entire investments and the saving for the people for their future. Other than keeping a home a better place through proper house-keeping jobs, one must also focus on the etiquettes and the interpersonal behaviour with the other family members and neighbours. Good behaviour helps in maintaining good relations with people around us.

In a narrow sense, house-keeping refers to general cleaning and maintenance in a clinical environment. The purpose of house-keeping is to reduce the number of micro-organisms at the site, thus reducing the risk of infection and accidents, and to provide an appealing space to all.

An appealing environment contributes to members' satisfaction, making them likely to be more productive in their work environment and more pleasing in person. A more pleasant environment improves client satisfaction.

In this book we will be focusing on the various areas related to home affairs. The areas related to home which can help today's women to perform better in their busy schedule. We will provide useful and tried tips to make home a great place.

Advantages of Good House-keeping

- Less clutter and rubbish (these are the most common causes of injury and unpleasantness)
- You can find what you are looking for quicker (improved efficiency and production and less frustration)
- Neat space (more enjoyable and comfortable to stay in)

Key Steps to Good House-keeping

Cleaning house, while necessary for all, is a very personal issue. Don't worry about other people's standards. Decide what 'clean' means to you and keep your house accordingly.

Establish Priorities

Identify which tasks have to be done absolutely, which ones should be done and which ones would be nice to get done. Work on them in that order and forget about all others.

Set Time Limits

You can accomplish quite a bit in several 10- or 20-minute periods. Keep your cleaning schedule flexible, so you can change it if something unexpected comes up. Do what you can when you can.

Delegate

Teach your kids how to fold laundry, vacuum, dust, unload the dishwasher, make their beds and prepare their breakfasts, lunches and snacks. Ask your teens to help with big jobs like washing windows and floors and cleaning cabinets and woodwork.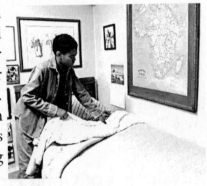

Finish Tasks

Complete one project before you start another.

Two-Timing

Make double use of your time — straighten the coat closet while waiting for the car pool, clean kitchen counters while talking on the telephone, etc.

A Family Affair

Set aside at least two hours once or twice a week for cleaning. Write down all necessary tasks on slips of paper and put them in a bowl according to difficulty.

Every family member chooses from the bowl. Enforce the rule that everyone helps with some cleaning task during that time.

Spill Savvy

Wipe up spills as soon as possible. The sooner you clean up, the easier it is to remove stains completely.

Minimize Spring-Cleaning

Clean as needed. Systematic, regular cleaning minimizes the need for heavy-duty seasonal cleaning.

You can keep your house cleaner by preventing outdoor dirt from getting in. Use doormats and boot scrapers. As needed, sweep sidewalks, steps and stairwells leading to your home.

If you have the space, set up a mudroom, where wet and soiled clothing and boots can be removed and stored. To reduce airborne dust, regularly vacuum registers and radiators.

Change the filters in your air conditioners and furnace, following the manufacturer's instructions. If you have severe allergies, hire a professional yearly to clean heating and ventilation ducts to reduce dust and molds.

Handy Tips for House-keeping

For some, work in the house seems to be never-ending. Here are some tips to help you tackle the task and put your home in order.

A housekeeper's job is often a never-ending one. It is a routine, thankless job. With more and more ladies taking up jobs outside the home, it becomes imperative that the entire family pitches in to create a homely atmosphere. Here are a few tips to help you tackle the job and put your home and consequently your life in order.

Importance of Delegating

Women often prefer to do everything themselves. This is because they feel that a certain job is to be done in a certain way and only they can do it perfectly. They don't pass on the responsibility to other family members and feel cheated when no one lifts a finger to help. In reality, when all the members of the family work together, chores can be done in a fraction of time and everyone can have the satisfaction of having contributed something towards the maintenance of their homes.

Match the Job to the Person

Each member of the family should be asked to take up a particular task. The important thing is to make sure that the task is suitable for their age and their interests. If your husband is a couch potato he can cut vegetables and fruits while watching his favourite TV show. Similarly your son, who is always on the go, can be asked to run a few errands. However, if you ask him to peel the garlic he may not be so cooperative simply because it is not in his nature to stay put in a place for more than five minutes.

Ask for Help

Whether it is your spouse, your kids or your in-laws, asking for help always fetches the desired result rather. However, at the same time, avoid bossing around. It is a good idea to sit with family members and prepare a list of jobs to be done. Most of the times people don't understand the volume of work involved, and hence may not come forward to do things. But once you have it in black and white, everyone can pitch in. Try to swap places for a day. Let your kids be the parent for a day and you do the role of the kid. While they enjoy the new role, they will also understand the hard work it involves.

Make it Fun

On holidays when you expect your kids to clean their rooms or their cupboards, switch on their favourite music. Get a pack of popcorns and get them started. Everyone will be a lot more cooperative. Don't forget to shower praises. Even if the job is not done perfectly, don't make them redo it, as by doing so you would be killing their enthusiasm. Later, when they are in a listening mood you can gently point out the mistakes, so the next time around they can correct themselves. It is better to give the instructions in a friendly tone before they start the job, or to help them do it the first few times until they get the hang of it.

■ ■ ■

CHAPTER 2

Manage your Home

Realise importance of having a simple, organised home, and take steps toward creating an atmosphere that aids home relaxation, and have your home the way you want it. This way, you'll want to hold onto the sense of peace and order you've created. It's easy for busy people to backslide into messy surroundings after a few weeks, so the following steps may be needed to guard the gains you've made:

Clean Regularly

This sounds like the obvious solution to having a mess, but it's not always easy to do when you have a busy life. However, if you keep a schedule and clean a different room of the house every few days, and do a 'clean sweep' before you go to bed each night, you can keep your surroundings clean with minimal effort.

Stay Organised

As you accumulate new things, be sure you're also regularly donating and tossing things you no longer use. Also, be sure everything you own has a 'home', so you can put things away quickly and find things easily.

Hire a Helper

You may also want to have someone clean your house once a week or twice a month, which will help you feel like you're not alone in your efforts, and make it easier to keep things clean the rest of the time. Having peaceful surroundings can give you a sense of peace that comes from having a haven from the outside world. Here are some additional tips for creating and maintaining a Low-Stress Zone in your home:

Create Peaceful Zones

If you haven't already, you may want to continue organising and decorating your space as time goes on. Perhaps you can create a place for journaling or meditation, perhaps a home spa area in your bathroom, or a space for yoga practice in your living room. Think of what areas you would have in an ideal vacation spot, and see if you can re-create them in your home.

Use your Machine

Do you find dinner, conversations, and leisure time interrupted by the phone? If you want some peace in the evenings, don't be afraid to let phone calls go to the answering machine or voice mail. It might feel strange at first to just let calls go unanswered when you're home, but you may be surprised by how much stress you can avoid when you're not jumping up to get the phone all the time when you're trying to rest. Be good about getting back to people, and they shouldn't mind.

Avoid Telemarketers and Junk Mail

If you haven't already, get yourself on the Do Not Call list. This can greatly reduce or eliminate the amount of annoying calls you receive from telemarketers. And if you find yourself buried under an avalanche of junk mail, writing to these people would be a really good idea. You can really cut down on the amount of mail you have to sort through and shred, which will also reduce more stress than you may realize.

Automatic Bill Payment

Another thing you can do to cut down on mail and save yourself time is to sign up for automatic bill payment. Many of your bills can be deducted from your checking account each month, or at least paid online, which will cut down on time spent writing checks mailing letters, and money spent on postage.

Don't Stress Over a Little Mess

If you have small children or another situation that makes keeping a clean house especially difficult, give yourself permission to have a little clutter.

While it's great to have minimal clutter, sometimes stressing about an inevitable amount of mess can cause more stress. So, work toward order, but don't obsess.

Management for Cleaning Schedule

Creating a cleaning schedule can be a confusing job. How often do cleaning tasks need to be performed? How long does a particular job take? What chores are considered daily, weekly, monthly, or seasonal tasks? The truth is that no one schedule will work perfectly for two different people. If your home has small children, you may find that weekly tasks need to be performed daily to prevent getting behind. If you live alone, some daily tasks may only need to be done weekly. Allergy sufferers, and people with breathing issues may need to perform certain tasks on a more frequent basis. Use the following guidelines as a starting point to developing your own daily, weekly, monthly, and seasonal cleaning schedule.

Daily Cleaning Chores

Daily cleaning chores are the absolute minimum that must be done on a daily basis to keep a home clean. Depending on the type of household you live in, some of these chores may even need to be done more than once during a day.

Clean Dishes

Cleaning dishes daily is the best choice all around. Smells, stains, and odd fungal growth usually go with forgotten dirty dishes.

Wash Laundry

Not every family needs to wash laundry daily, but many of us find that at least a daily load of laundry is necessary. With work clothes, school uniforms, soccer practice clothes, and sports uniforms, our families can generate a lot of dirty clothes. A daily load can help prevent a mad dash.

Tidy Up

Doing a little clutter control on a daily basis will keep your home ready for company at a moment's notice. A few minutes of picking up each day also prevent your home from turning into a disaster zone that will take hours to plow through. A tidy room makes a big difference in one's motivation to tackle bigger projects. Use the '15-Minute cleanups' as a daily help to keep your main rooms ready for visitors.

Weekly Cleaning Chores

Although most of these chores don't require daily work, they are still some of the most important tasks that need to be done in our homes. Some items may need to be completed more often. Scheduling these chores in addition to your daily chores will help you maintain order and cleanliness in your home.

Vacuuming

Vacuuming your home on a weekly basis prevents buildups of dust that can trigger allergies and respiratory issues for your family and guests.

While high traffic areas may need to be vacuumed on a daily basis, other areas of the home need a good once-over once a week. Vacuuming flooring adds years to the life of your floors.

Don't Forget to Vacuum...

- Carpets
- Rugs
- Stairs
- Furniture
- Hard floors

Dusting

Through no fault of our home, dust collects on every surface, leading to breathing issues, dull looking surfaces, and the need to dust weekly. A good weekly dusting staves off the need for more in depth cleaning on a regular basis.

Be sure to dust from top to bottom to prevent settling. Consider using a vacuum attachment to suck up the dust, or a good microfibre cloth to trap dust particles.

Don't Forget to Dust...

- Furniture
- Windowsills
- Wall Coverings
- Cobwebs
- Ceiling Fans

Cleaning

There are some areas of our homes that are not use frequently. They need to be tended to on a weekly basis. This preventative cleaning keeps these rooms and areas ready to serve our home, and keeps buildups of dirt and damage from requiring more intense cleaning later.

Don't Forget to...

- Clean Entry and patio doors
- Shake out door mats
- Straighten books and magazines
- Clean bathrooms
- Change linens in all rooms
- Clean kitchen sink
- Clean toaster
- Clean stovetops
- Wipe down kitchen appliances
- Clean microwave (inside and out)
- Clean Walls
- Clean leftovers from fridge
- Gather and take out trash

Monthly Cleaning Chores

Monthly cleaning chores can be favourite weekend chores. These are areas of your home that can afford to be neglected during your daily and weekly cleaning sessions, but ultimately a good thorough monthly cleaning is needed.

Dust Ceiling Fans

If it has been awhile since you've cleaned your ceiling fan, take a look up. You're likely to see a ton of dust and dirt clinging to your ceiling fans. Dust the ceiling fan at least once a month to keep it looking nice and functioning well.

Clean Light Fixtures

Cleaning light fixtures on a monthly basis keeps your globes and fixtures from dulling and becoming encrusted with dust and bug remains.

Dust Air Vents

You may not notice the air vents in your home regularly, but they can quickly buildup dust around the vent and wall areas. Dust them down monthly to keep dust from blowing out into your rooms.

Clean Walls

Even families without small children will discover occasional marks on the walls of their home. Clean the walls of your home to remove crayon marks, furniture scuffs, dust, and splatters. Food preparation, eating areas, and the place you store your trash will be likely candidates for a monthly wall wipe-down.

Clean Window Treatments

Curtains and drapes may need to be washed, cleaned, or dusted out on a monthly basis. Blinds that attract dust will need to be wiped down as well. Be sure to check the manufacturer's instructions for your window treatments before cleaning.

Dust Intensively

Besides the quick dusting that you do on a daily and weekly basis, more intensive dusting needs to be done monthly. Dust behind furniture pieces and appliances. Dust window sills, ceilings, and baseboards. Don't forget to dust down doors, molding, and hidden corners were cobwebs may form.

Vacuum Inside Furniture

You can never know how so much stuff finds its way into the depths of the sofa. A monthly cleaning and vacuuming is likely to reveal many long lost items, and quite a bit of dirt. Go down into the crevices to pull out items that need to be kept. Next, vacuum out the inside of the couch.

Clean Windows

A monthly cleaning for windows includes cleaning the inside of the glass and wiping down the windowsills. Use a glass cleaner to remove streaks and spots on the interior of the windows. If you wait for an overcast day, you'll reduce the streaking and spotting on the glass.

Spot Treat Carpet and Upholstery

Check for spots on the carpet and upholstery and spot treat the stains. Be sure to test the stain treater in an inconspicuous spot before applying liberally. If it's been awhile since your carpet was last cleaned, it may be time to schedule a shampooing.

Check Smoke Alarms

If you have a smoke alarm installed, double check that it is functioning properly. Change the batteries if needed. Be sure to dust down the smoke alarm to keep it in working order.

Change Filters

To keep your air conditioner running smoothly, you'll need to change the filter monthly. This is a good time to check your vacuum cleaner filters and clean or replace them.

Deep Clean Appliances

Home appliances take a lot of abuse. At least once a month, treat them to a deep cleaning that renews them to their original glory. Use a good oven cleaner to remove baked on drips and overflows from your oven.

Remove everything from your refrigerator and freezer and wipe them down thoroughly. Toss any outdated food. Be sure to place new boxes of baking soda in both to help control odours. Scrub down the inside and outside of your microwave oven.

Seasonal Cleaning Chores

Although seasonal cleaning chores are important, they are usually the most forgotten parts of home maintenance. Your attention is only needed in these areas two to three times a year, but it is vital to maintaining and cleaning our homes.

Six Steps of Success for Home

Sort Out and Dispose

Elimination of unnecessary things helps in organising the things. Only those items are kept that are needed.

Undertake major cleaning and also save money on buying unnecessary additional storage equipment and space.

Place for Everything and Everything in Place

Establishing a neat layout to fix storage places and the methods, and stick to the rules. This helps in eliminating search time and therefore, stresses and strains.

Saving money by not purchasing the items now easily available at home.

Manage Time

Understanding that cleanliness is a form of inspection and establishing state of cleanliness commensurate to our needs.

Involvement of every individual results in achieving zero grime and zero dirt. For this, giving a definite time each day for cleaning is good option.

Standardise the Methods

Establish standards for maintaining. Add colour and use innovative visible management so that abnormalities show up for early action.

Environmental Upkeep

Contributing to environmental upkeep is another way to make the house a better place.

Self Discipline and Training

Feel accountable and set examples to maintain the established procedures of orderliness and neatness. Full participation in developing and practicing good habits is needed from every member.

Adopting the above mentioned house-keeping tips helps in making us more and more experienced. They are astronishing advantages as we start implementing the six steps of success.

- Home looks clean, tidy and beautiful.
- Feels great to live in such a home.
- Impresses everyone.
- Improves hygiene at home.
- No one at home wastes any time in searching and retrieving the things.
- Home is a safe place now.
- The environment around is clean and healthy.
- There is no clutter around.
- There is no need to spend money to procure additional storage space or equipment for that clutter.
- Saves lots of money.

With the thought of the management of the home, it sounds like a big job. But it will be much easier if you cut the task and use the principle- 'Divide and Rule'.

Organising Work

After realising that you have stuffs which you do not need or want, you've taken a giant step in the right direction. That fact alone will make that job easier. Follow these tips and then you are on the way to an organised home:

- Decide first on what room to start on.
- Write all to do work on a paper.
- Designate an appropriate reward to give yourself on the dumping portion of the job.
- Set a specific dumping completion deadline for this one room.
- Schedule 3 specific dumping dates (one hour for each).
- Paste this action sheet in a prominent place where you would look at it everyday. It will serve as a reminder for your goal, deadline and dumping reward.
- When the first dumping date day arrives, keep that appointment.
- Bring a bunch of large garbage bags.
- Set a timer for one hour- one that sounds off when the hour is up.
- Pick up one item at a time, and start dumping.
- Continue doing this until the timer goes off.
- If you prefer to continue, keep going.
- Don't let the garbage bags sit there.
- Make sure they are thrown out.
- Once you've managed to dump everything you don't want in that room. It's time to celebrate.

Apart from organising the households, there are some other important tips which are helpful in organising the home. Some basic do's are important and thus play an important role in maintaining a good house-keeping. The tasks related to organising the households are:

- Observe where certain stuff accumulates and design the house around that rather than trying to get your family to fit your systems.

- If space allows, have one room that is your 'good' or clean room. Have no toys in there and no food or drink at any time.

- Have a nice wicker basket in every single room in the house. Use it for chucking in any toys that are on the floor of that room.

- Have a shoe box in the hall, or porch or utility room - don't even try a show rack.

- Have a place for your house/car keys. Put them in the same place every single time; it will eventually become a habit.

- Never underestimate the power of flowers. Pop a bunch of fresh flowers in the room where you spend the most time and you will find your eyes drawn to them rather than the less attractive stains and scuffs.

- Keep a bottle of washing-up liquid and a cloth in your bathroom and every day squirt and wipe round the sink, bath and shower.

  It takes maybe one or two minutes at most and you'll find you never have to 'clean' the bathroom.

- Spend ten minutes on one non-essential job every day. It is amazing how doing these jobs adds up to a clutter-free home.

Don't tackle 'a room' or 'the house'. Just do this one small extra job each day.

- Let the light in. It is amazing how much extra light a cleaned window lets in and the light brightens and freshens up everything in the home.

- Remember these wise words- 'If in doubt, throw it out' and 'If it's not beautiful or useful, get rid of it'.

■ ■ ■

CHAPTER 3

Cleaning the House

While following the various house-keeping tips starting from the cleaning of the house to maintaining the interpersonal relationships with the neighbours, cleanup is a brief step-by-step guide to cleaning every corner of a house. While the rooms may not be white glove clean, they will be presentable to guests. Cleanups are a great way to maintain a home in between more thorough cleanings.

A home that is free of clutter and clean is more spacious, attractive, and healthy than a house that needs a good cleaning all the time. Freshly washed floors, beds that are made, and gleaming windows are just some of the perks that make a clean house a great place to be.

Unfortunately, even though everyone loves a clean house, not everyone can find the time to put into keeping it clean. It takes a lot of work, and it does always seem that the job is never done.

When you have a home that you love when it is clean but don't have the time for the upkeep, there are pretty much two options that you have. You can hire a house cleaning service or you can keep on doing (or not doing) your routine now, which is probably squeezing in time for the house whenever you can manage.

Unfortunately we lose a lot of free time because of house work, which means less time to do the things that we actually want to do. Hiring a housekeeper, maid, or service can free up hours of time every week since you wont have to do the things that take up so much of that time.

Most people absolutely love having a service come in and clean the house for them. They love to come home from a hard day at work to a sparkling home, without having to do it all themselves. The money spent is well worth it to them, and they wouldn't trade it for the world.

However, there are some people that don't think that hiring a cleaning staff is right for them. Some say that it makes them feel lazy, and others are embarrassed by their mess and they feel like they have to apologize to the cleaner for having them clean up so much stuff, even though that is their job.

However, most people really enjoy leaving the dirty work to someone else.

For those people who feel like they need to find a better way to clean without hiring someone, there is hope! There are some tricks that you can try to make things not only go faster, but you'll be more efficient when you are picking up the house, too. All it takes 10 minutes and you might be surprised at what you can do in that little amount of time.

There are tons of little jobs that can be done in ten minutes, like choosing one thing in the house to dust, such as a certain bookshelf, etc. You can take ten minutes and just tidy up the bathroom. Forget the whole bathroom and just clean a toilet bowl real quick. You can take just a few minutes and pick up the dirty clothes that the kids have just tossed on the floor.

Even though doing these things won't turn your home from dingy to dazzling, if you do this for six days of the week, by the time the day comes for you to spend some real time doing a deeper cleaning job, you'll have shaved off an entire hour off of the time that it takes you to accomplish this. Cleaning the house doesn't have to be done all at one time!

However, quick cleanup is not the only cleaning regimen one needs to keep the home in tip top shape. It's not an intense cleaning, but only a brief pickup of a room. To really keep a home clean, more thorough work will need to be done according to the cleaning schedule.

Before intensely cleaning a room, it's a good idea to start with that room's quick cleanup, which lastly gives the perfect face of the entire house.

Cleanup Works

Cleanup works because it recognises that there are three types of items we need to clean up in a room. Everything falls into one of three categories.

1. **Trash:** Those items which do not belong to the room and are waste.

2. **Things that don't belong in the room:** Those items which are not relevant to the room and are not part of the room.

3. **Things that belong in the room, in a different place:** Those items which are the part of the room but are spread everywhere, i.e they are not placed at their proper place.

The various cleanups for various places include the main parts of the house, thus giving a good look to the home.

Major Cleanup Areas

Some major cleanups of the home include:

Living Area Cleanup

This cleanup can work for formal and informal living areas and sitting areas. It also works for formal dining rooms, and other rooms where entertaining is done. The idea with this cleanup is to get the room ready for guests, or events without spending a lot of time on the details.

Kitchen Cleanup

The kitchen cleanup aims to remove trash, dirty dishes, and unwanted items from a kitchen, making it ready to be used, or in good shape for guests to be around. While you won't scrub out the refrigerator, or clean under the sink in this cleanup, you will remove any offending trash and dishes, making your kitchen clean and clutter free.

Bathroom Cleanup

The bathroom cleanup helps you quickly organise and wipe down bathroom surfaces. This cleanup will work to maintain your weekly bathroom scrub down, or get a bathroom ready in a hurry when unexpected guests show up.

Kid's Room Cleanup

This kid's room cleanup is great for parents at a loss for where to begin when faced with a disaster area child's room.

Bedroom Cleanup

Most people leave cleaning their own bedroom for last. After a busy day or week, a bedroom can be in terrible shape. This cleanup will help maintain a bedroom or give it a quick pickup just in time for a restful night.

Dorm Room Cleanup

The dorm room cleanup is for those who live in a very small area like an efficiency apartment, or campus housing. These small places can quickly fill up with junk and trash, but this quick cleanup will help organise even the worst-case scenario.

Room-by-Room House-Cleaning Tips

Kitchen

- Wipe up spills in the refrigerator as soon as you notice them, and if you have time, do the rest of the shelf or any gloppy jar bottoms.
- Go through just one refrigerator or pantry shelf and toss anything that's past the expiration date, that you'll never use again or that's less than a single serving.
- Toss the jumble of unused takeout disposable containers, glass jars and condiment packages you've collected.
- Wipe fingerprints of all the kitchen cabinets.
- Cut time when polishing the floors. Apply the wax with a long-handled paint roller.

- As you cook, rinse dirty utensils, pots and pans and put them in the dishwasher. You'll have the kitchen in good order when you sit down to eat, and you'll have less to clean up after dinner.

- Ease the weekday morning rush by setting the table for breakfast before you go to bed. Put out cereal boxes, sweeteners and other nonperishable items. Prepare the coffeemaker and set the timer.

- If the dishwasher's not full, add burner covers or small shelves from the refrigerator — anything that needs washing.

- While you're talking on the phone or waiting on endless hold, clean out five to seven unwanted, unused things from the kitchen junk drawer or pantry or your purse.

Bathroom

- Store a floor duster with disposable cloths in a closet near the bathroom. It will be easy to grab the duster and go over the floor during the week.

- If you use disposable makeup cloths to wash your face, rinse and reuse them to quick-clean the sink, counter or floor.

- After your family finishes brushing their teeth or shaving, use a dry terrycloth hand towel on the mirror and bathroom faucets to wipe away spots of lather so they won't build up.

- Before getting out of the shower, clean the stall or tub and tiles with a squeegee.

- After you flush the toilet, sprinkle 1/4 cup of baking soda into the wet bowl. Take your shower and then give the bowl a single scrub. Flush to rinse.

Family Room

- Go through magazine and catalogue piles and discard outdated issues, three or five at a time. Toss junk mail daily.

- Vacuum just the high-traffic sections of the floor or carpet and do the other areas later.

- Before you go to bed, do a fast pickup. Put remote controls in a basket, tidy newspapers and loose papers or put them in the trash, clean off the coffee table, plump pillows and fold throws.

- When you're done vacuuming the floor and baseboards, use the upholstery attachment to dust one bookshelf.

- If your children's plastic toys look dirty, grab the worst two or three and clean them with a wet wipe or a paper towel moistened with rubbing alcohol.

- Quick-clean artificial flowers with the upholstery attachment of the vacuum cleaner.

- To freshen throw pillows, put them in the dryer, one or two at a time, on the air cycle.

- Vacuum lamp shades (turn off lamp before you dust) and the back of the TV.

Laundry

- To avoid a huge weekend laundry day, try to do at least a couple of loads of towels or clothes during the week.

- Cut laundry time by presorting items into baskets labelled towels, jeans, darks, lights, etc.

- Before you do a load of wash, wipe off the front and sides of the washer and dryer with a damp cloth (then launder the cloth). Clear the lint filter with a comb.

- Organise freshly washed linens into sets. Fold flat sheets in half the long way and then in half along the long fold (repeat fold for wider sheets).

  Do the same with the fitted sheets, laying each on top of a folded flat sheet. Fold the matching pillowcases in half (the long way too), lay them on top of the sheets and roll everything into one neat set. Stack on shelves. This way, each family member can grab the set for his or her bed.

Bedroom

- When vacuuming the bedroom, take a few extra moments to clean under the bed so the dust bunnies won't multiply.

- While you get dressed in the morning, check your nightstand or dresser top and pick three to five items to toss out (ticket stubs, empty perfume bottles, for example).

  Clean the phone with an alcohol-based wipe or go through one drawer in your dresser, weeding out items you no longer wear or want.

- Shorten the stack of bedside reading material by moving items you want to save back to the bookshelf or file cabinet and getting the rest ready for recycling.

- If you don't have time for a thorough dusting, go over curtains, mini-blinds and the headboard with the upholstery attachment of your vacuum.

- To save steps in making beds, store an extra set of sheets under the mattress. If you have a sofa bed, store linens and a bed pillow inside one of the pillow shams on the couch.

Quick Review of House-Cleaning Tasks

- For cleaning a house, you need to dedicate a lot of time. So, the first step would be to decide how much time you are going to spend on cleaning.

- Once the time is set, get started by looking into the areas of concern. You would find that there are a number of things you need to look into, while cleaning a house.

- Start with the glass windows and mirrors. For this, take some warm water in a bucket and add to it some soap to make a foamy solution.

  Now, pick up a sponge and start cleaning all the glass panes and mirrors. Wash it with plain water and dry the glass with newspaper. Your windows and mirrors would be gleaming with lustre!

- Now, turn to the furniture at your house. While some can be cleaned with a soapy solution, there are others that might get worn out. For the latter, rubbing with a dry cloth would serve as the good option. Dust the cushions and set them on the sofa. As for the dining table, properly keep the place-mats, serving dishes, if any.

- Once the above is done, switch to the laundry. If you have a large pile of clothes, wash them in turns with the whites in the beginning and coloured clothes later.

- Drying the clothes is as important as washing them. Set them neatly on the wires outside, with all the clothes properly hanging. Make sure you fasten them with clothes pin.

- For those of you who have children at home, make sure you put all their toys in the toy chest.

- Once the clothes and toys are neatly organised, start

cleaning the floors. Start with the first room and head along the home. Vacuuming serves as the most effective way for cleaning up all the dust and junk that accumulates on your floor. For tiled or wooden flooring, dry dust mops would be the best bet.

- Do not forget to mop the floor as well. This would clean the house further, making it look neat and tidy.

- Come to the kitchen, now. Stuff all the small dishes in the dishwasher and run it. As for the bigger pots and pans, the most appropriate option would be to hand-wash them. Place the thoroughly rinsed dishes in a clean drying rack and allow to air dry.

- Clean the counter-top of the kitchen and organise everything neatly in the racks and cupboards.

- Once the kitchen is done, turn to the washrooms. Start with the toilet seat and then move to the floor and tiles. Use a mild detergent for the purpose. Do not forget to clean the wash basin as well.

- Now, all you need to do is take a warm water bath and relax yourself in your neat and tidy home!

Top 5 Alternate Home Cleaners

Instead of buying expensive household cleaners, using these common and inexpensive household products can be an effective and frugal way to cut your cleaning expenses. These are alternate products to have on hand to take care of almost every household cleaning need.

1. Baking Soda

Baking soda, or sodium bicarbonate, is a natural substance that neutralizes both acids and bases, so it eliminates odours rather than just covering them up. In cooking, baking soda releases carbon dioxide when heated, and this causes cookies, breads or cakes to rise.

Baking soda can also act as an abrasive cleaner perfect for removing stains from sinks, counter tops and even fine china.

2. White Vinegar

Vinegar is an inexpensive cleaner, good for removing hard water deposits, shining glass, windows and most metal surfaces. It can also remove stains and mildew. Use in your coffeemaker to keep it brewing quickly.

3. Bleach

Bleach is best known as a fabric whitener. It also disinfects bathrooms and kitchens, and kills mildew and mold.

4. Borax

Borax is also known as a laundry booster; add a handful to your washer to help your detergent work better. Also deodourizes garbage pails and disposers, cleans and whitens walls and floors, and cleans cookware.

5. WD-40

WD-40, a petroleum-based lubricant and cleaner, has many household uses beyond the garage. Among the many household uses for WD-40 are crayon and adhesive removal, grease and grime cleaning and lubricating metal parts throughout your house.

Feeling the Urge to Clean?

Look at each room and identify specific tasks. Make a list of cleaning priorities. Share the fun with family members.

- **Kitchen:** wash and wax wood floors and mop vinyl floors. Clean out refrigerator and pantry. Change shelf-liners. Straighten junk drawer wipe down cabinet.

- **Bathroom:** Use lint-free cloths or a squeegee to wash windows inside and out. Dust the sill. Vacuum the window well.

- **Window Treatments:** Vacuum draperies. Wash blinds. Replace heavy drapes with lightweight or sheer curtains.

- **Furniture:** Polish furniture, wash upholstery, vacuum between cushions. Clean behind and under sofas and cabinets.

- **Closets:** Give old clothes and furniture to charity. Vacuum floors. Dust shelves. Hang cedar blocks to freshen the areas.

Best Way to Tackle Cleaning

- Always start at the top of the room and work your way down.

- Always clean top to bottom. When you dust, start at the top and work down.

- Take all your cleaning tools with you into each room to avoid unnecessary trips back and forth.

- Unplug the phone and turn off the T.V.

- Eliminate clutter. An uncluttered home looks better than one that is dust-free but strewn with odds and ends.

- Clean as you go! It takes a lot less time to remove new dirt than old, and to clean and put away stuff as you use it, than to clean and store the pile-up you can accumulate.

- A house that smells fresh will give the impression of cleanliness. Leave baking soda on carpeting for the night to absorb musty odours, vacuum in the morning.

- Keep a big astro-turf mat on the porch to cut down on tracked in dirt.

- Keep a basket in the kitchen for the mail, newspaper, car keys to help with clutter.

- Keep a hamper in every bathroom.

- Make everyone in charge of making his or her own bed and picking up their stuff.

- Always pickup the T.V. room before bedtime and start the dishwasher.

- Prioritize, if your time is limited decide what is most important.

- Delegate, get the entire family involved.

- Make a checklist, when a job is completed, check it off - you'll feel as though you are really accomplishing something.

Cleaning Tips for Different Areas

Clean Doors Give a Great Impression

If company is coming, clean and wash the doors in your house. With clean doors, your whole house will look good. Scrub the door from top to bottom with a rag and soapy water, using a scrub brush for especially tough spots. While you're at it, wipe down the top edge of the frame. With all the dust that collects up there, it probably looks like velvet. Along with the upper side of a ceiling fan, the top of the door is one of the most missed spots in the home.

Blood Stains

- Put a paste of water and cornstarch, cornmeal or talcum powder on fresh spots. Let dry and brush off.

- Cover fresh or dried stains with meat tenderizer and add cool water. After 15 to 30 minutes, sponge off with cool water.

- If handling fresh blood on leather, dab on a little hydrogen peroxide. After it bubbles, wipe it off.

- If you get blood on fabric, quickly wet a long piece of white cotton thread with saliva and place it across the spot. The thread will absorb the blood.

Removing Crayon Marks

Remove crayon marks from painted walls by scrubbing with toothpaste or an ammonia-soaked cloth. Rinse and dry.

Removing Heel Marks

Take pencil eraser and rub them off.

Quick Fix for Shiny Wood Floors

Put a piece of waxed paper under your dust mop. Dirt will stick to the mop and the wax will shine your floors.

Cleaning Windows

- If necessary, dust off the window and sill with a clean paintbrush. Excess dust and water can cause mud.

- Use a professional-type squeegee.

- Don't clean windows while they are in direct sunlight. Your cleaning solution will dry too fast.

- Dip a 100% cotton cleaning cloth in your solution. Wring out the excess and then wipe the window to loosen dirt.

- Grab your squeegee. Start each squeegee stroke in a dry spot. Wipe a strip with a cleaning cloth to get started.

- Squeegee in a pattern from top to bottom, or side to side. If you clean the outside and the inside, work top to bottom on the inside and side to side on the  outside. By doing this, you'll be able to identify which side any streaks left behind are on.

- Keep the squeegee blade dry by wiping it with a cleaning cloth after each stroke.

- Replace the blade when necessary. Even the smallest nick can cause streaking.

- Don't have a squeegee? Use newspaper for drying freshly washed windows. It's cheaper and leaves no lint behind.

More Window Washing Hints

Wash windows on a cloudy, but not rainy day. This is the best time to vacuum the frames and sills. Cool, clear water is the choice of most professional window washers. If windows are very dirty you can add 2 to 3 tablespoons of vinegar per gallon of water. For drying windows, a wad of crumpled newspaper works just as well as expensive paper towels.

Wear rubber gloves to keep your hands free of ink. To remove spots, rub the surface with rubbing alcohol.

Removing Tar Spots

Use paste wax to remove tar from floors. This works on shoes too.

Candle Wax

- For spilled wax on carpets and upholstery, put a brown paper bag over the dried wax and run a hot iron over it. The bag will absorb the hot wax.
- Dried wax on wood floors can be removed by softening the wax with a hair dryer, then removing with paper towels. Wash spot down with a combination of vinegar and water.

Cleaning Soiled Shirt Collars

Take a small paintbrush and brush hair shampoo into soiled shirt collars before laundering. Shampoo is made to dissolve body oils.

Cleaning Combs and Brushes

Use a combination of baking soda and hot water to clean hair brushes and combs.

Removing Deodorant Stains from Washables

Sponge area with white vinegar. If stain remains, soak with denatured alcohol. Wash with detergent in hottest water safe for fabric.

Cleaning Glass Table Tops

- Clean by rubbing with a little lemon juice, dry with paper towels and polish with newspaper for a sparkling table.

- Toothpaste will remove small scratches from glass.

Cleaning Marble

To remove stains, sprinkle salt on a fresh cut lemon. Rub very lightly over stain. Do not rub hard or you will ruin the polished surface. Wash off with soap and water.

Polishing Furniture

- Carved furniture- dip old toothbrush into furniture polish and brush lightly.

- To remove polish build-up mix one cup water and one cup vinegar. Dip soft cloth in the mixture and wring out before wiping furniture. Dry immediately with another soft, dry cloth.

Cleaning Acoustical Tiles

- Clean with the dust-brush attachment of your vacuum cleaner.

- Remove stains and dirt with mild soap and water. Don't let the tiles get too wet.

Cleaning Wallpaper

- To dust papered walls, tie a dustcloth over your broom and work from the top down.

- To remove pencil marks and other non-greasy spots from non-washable papers, use an art-gum eraser or a slice of fresh rye bread.

- To remove greasy spots, crayon marks and food stains,

apply a paste of cleaning fluid and fuller's earth, cornstarch or whiting. Let dry and brush off. Repeat the treatment until the spot is gone.

- Wipe off fingerprints with a damp cloth, then sprinkle the moist area with fuller's earth. Let it dry and then brush it off.

- To prevent splash marks when you're washing baseboards or other woodwork, mask wallpaper with a wide ruler, venetian blind-slat or a piece of rigid plastic.

- When you save scraps of wallpaper for patching, tack them to a wall in the attic or closet. When you use them for repairs, they won't look so brand new.

Removing Water Stains

- If the fabric is non-washable, gently scratch off the stain (which is made up of mineral deposits) with your fingernail. Still there? Hold the spot over a steaming teakettle until well-dampened. As it dries, rub the stain, working from its outer edges toward the centre.

- Remove hard-water stains from glasses and bottles by rubbing them with steel wool dipped in vinegar.

- Cover hard-water stains on bathroom fixtures with a paste of baking soda and vinegar. Then drape with a terry clot towel and let stand for about an hour. Wipe off, rinse and dry.

Cleaning Wicker

Remove dust from wicker by vacuuming with the dust brush attachment. To remove grime, wash with a solution of 2 tablespoons ammonia per gallon of water. Use a paintbrush or a toothbrush to get at hard-to-reach places. Rinse well. Air dry in the shade.

Quick Cleaning of Miniblinds

- Slip your hands into a pair of socks for cleaning the miniblinds. Dip one hand into a bucket of warm, soapy water and hold the blinds between your two hands. Rub back and forth until you've cleaned the whole surface. Then reverse sides so the dry sock dries the blinds.

- Wipe miniblinds with damp fabric softener sheets to eliminate static that collects dust. The same trick works for your T.V. screen.

Miniblind Spring Cleaning

- Take the blind down and take it outside.

- Lay it on an old blanket preferably on a slanted area of the yard.

- Let the blind out all the way and make sure all the louvers are flat.

- Mix up a bucket of all-purpose cleaner or ammonia solution.

- Scrub with a soft brush then turn it over to do the back side.

- By now the blanket is wet and is helping to clean the blind and protecting it.

- Hang the blind on a clothesline and hose it off.

- Gentle shaking will help it begin to drip dry.

Cleaning Indoor Plants

Remember, plants get dusty too. You can clean small plants in the kitchen sink, and larger ones enjoy a shower in the bathroom.

Doorknobs

Always disinfect doorknobs, switchplates and telephones. They collect germs from everyone who touches them.

Clean Mirrors

Remove hair spray from a mirror with a little rubbing alcohol on a soft cloth.

Organise Linen Closets

Linen closets can be a jumbled mess, especially when you have children making their own beds. Organise bed linens in sets. Fold flat sheet in half twice lengthwise, then fold fitted sheet the same way and lay it on top of the flat folded sheet. Add one or two pillow cases folded long ways and roll them all together into a neat roll. Whoever is making the bed can grab only a roll instead of rummaging around and making a mess.

Dusting Tip

Spray broom or dust mop with your favourite furniture polish and the dust and dirt will be easier to collect when you sweep.

Fresh Curtains

Freshen curtains in the dryer with a fabric softener sheet and a damp towel.

Clean Cobwebs

If you can't reach the cobwebs with your feather duster, use the detached vacuum wand as an extension.

Clean Ashtrays

Spray furniture polish on hard to clean ashtrays. Ashes then dump out without sticking.

Odour and Moisture Removal

To get rid of odour you have to remove the source, not just cover the odour up with perfumed air freshener. Clean up and disinfect. Kill the germs that cause most household odours. The quicker you get after odours, the easier they are to remove.

Mix your Own Cleaning Solutions

- Ammonia, diluted with 3 parts water in an empty spray bottle can be used to clean windows, appliances and countertops. Full strength it can remove wax build-up from the kitchen floor.

- An excellent way to scour copper and brass is 1/2 cup vinegar mixed with 1 tablespoon salt.

- Full strength pine oil is great for deodourising garbage cans, and scrubbing the kitchen and bathroom floor.

- Baking soda can be used instead of scouring powder and also removes stains and odours from refrigerators and coffee pots.

- A sprinkle of dry baking soda before vacuuming will freshen the carpeting. Try it as a deodourizer for diaper pails and kitty litter.

Urine Spots

Get to them quickly with a solution of dish detergent and water.

If You've Got Allergies

- Air condition your home.

- Keep bathrooms free of mold and mildew.
- Avoid pets or restrict them to certain areas.
- Damp mop hard surfaces regularly.
- Enclose your fireplace.
- Fluff drapes and rugs in dryer to remove dust.
- Use your exhaust fans.
- Vacuum mattresses.
- Don't allow smoking in your home.
- Replace furnace filters frequently.
- Vacuum everything once a week.
- Invest in an ozone-free air cleaner.

■ ■ ■

CHAPTER 4

Maintaining Different Rooms

Maintenance of Living Room

Whether you live in a flat or rambling home, a cottage by the sea, or a house in town, your living room creates a lasting impression for all who enter. It tells your family and friends if you're formal and elegant or fun-loving and laid-back. It sets the mood for the home and should be a reflection of your personal taste.

A living room can be arranged in many ways. For some, this space is formal and perfect at all times, to be entered and used only when  guests come to call. To others, it serves as a comfortable family gathering place for watching TV, doing homework, or visiting. Some have a cozy snug for sipping tea and curling up with a book.

Pillows/Cushions

Throw pillows make a room feel comfortable. They are an easy and inexpensive way to change colour accents and add texture and colour warmth. A formal living room, historically referred to as a drawing room or parlor, often showcases the home owner's finest possessions. The decor is often symmetrical sofa with painting above, flanked by two end tables topped by lamps.

Formal window treatments of luxurious fabrics trimmed with braid and fringe, and perfectly set pairs of occasional chairs *and tables* follow traditional rules of decorating. Few homes these days have space for such a perfect (and often useless) room that is more to be looked at than used.

Home Lighting

Good lighting is the key to your decoration success. Attractive floor lamps with light coloured shades provide ambient light for the entire room. Table lamps highlight small decorating objects as well as providing concentrated light for reading, working and study.

Shades for small lamps can match your furnishings or be conversation pieces with a different colour and style.

Walls

Large areas, like walls, look best with a lighter colour. A darker or contrasting colour can be used on one wall for a dramatic effect. Beautiful paint makes pictures and decor 'pop' out of the background and increases their intensity. Try using warm colours like pink, peach or mauve. Or paint with soothing colours like blue or green. Remember, if you don't like it, you can always paint over it!

Furniture

Balance your room by placing large pieces of furniture around your living space. If possible, tall items like bookcases and grandfather clocks should be across from one another to keep the room from looking lop-sided. Add smaller pieces like tables in the spaces where they will be convenient and attractive.

If you have small furnishings or decorator objects, group them in uneven numbers, like one, three or five items together. Modern decoration style has evolved to allow a less formal look.

While retaining certain elements, such as beautiful millwork or lush fabrics, the more casual living room has lighter window treatments and more comfortable furniture.

Studied symmetry has given way to softer lines, fewer rules, and more colour. A more casual family room style of living room has a character of nonchalance. While furniture and fabrics should be coordinated, there are few rules. Choices are governed by practicality.

Furniture selection and placement is less structured. Seating around a TV is often necessary, with a table for casual eating. In a modern home, the living room may even have a computer centre, so a desk may have a place of prominence.

Regardless of what purpose your living room serves, the fabrics, colours, furniture, and accessories should be what you love. Whether it's serene and neutral, colourful and lively, or something in-between, it should reflect your taste.

Maintenance of Bedroom

Keeping bedroom clean and orderly will bring feelings of satisfaction and a room that is truly an escape from the chaos of life. The work you put into it is certainly worth the reward. And the work should not be that difficult if you follow this simple procedure: put everything in its  proper place, dust, vacuum, freshen, and maintain.

- Begin organising bedroom by putting everything there in its proper place.

- Dirty laundry should be put it in a hamper or taken to the laundry room.

- Drop your clothes directly into hamper each day.

- Hang up or fold your clean clothes and put them in your closet or bureau.

- Pick up stray books, magazines, mail, and other papers and decide what you will do with each one.

- If you're going to read it in the next 24 hours, place it where you will remember to read it.

- If you've already read it, put it in its proper place, either on a bookshelf, returned to the library, given away, or thrown away.

- If you haven't read it and don't plan on reading it in the next 24 hours, find a place to store it for future use. Place it on a bookshelf, in a drawer or basket, or create a new place to file it.

- Don't let a lot of clutter accumulate at your bedside.

- Take a look at your bureau and/or vanity.

- A pretty candy dish with a lid can be an inexpensive substitute for a jewellery box.

- If you eat snacks in the bedroom, be sure to return all plates, glasses, and flatware to the kitchen.

- If these things sit around too long, they not only add to the clutter, they can attract insects, cause odours, and breed mold and bacteria.

- Make the bed. At the very least, straighten the linens.

- This not only makes the room look neater, it also keeps the sheets and blankets fresh for a longer period of time by allowing them more access to the fresh air.

- The bed should be made up with fresh linens once a week.

- Finally, empty the trash bin.

- Place a garbage bin to toss unwanted papers, facial tissue, and other rubbish that you don't want in your living space.

Once everything is in its place, it is time to dust. You may find that as you become more organised, you can combine the task of dusting along with the task of putting things in their places.

While dusting, wipe all surfaces including window ledges, ceiling fans, and headboards and footboards on the bed. Check for cobwebs on the ceiling, especially near the walls and in the corners.

Work from the top down. Dust away the cobwebs first, then the shelves, then counter tops, and then lower items such as chairs and baseboards.

After dusting, it's time to vacuum. Before starting this step, take a look under your furniture. You don't want to suck up any lost buttons or valuable jewellery that may have fallen to the floor unnoticed. After this quick inspection, vacuum the entire floor, getting under the bed, bureau, desk, night stand, and behind the door. Seek out and suck up all of the "dust bunnies."

Now that your bedroom is clean, you may want to freshen the air a bit. If the weather permits, you may want to open your windows in order to let the fresh air circulate through the room. Briones also recommends lighting scented candles.

Once your room is in this clean, fresh condition, you will probably want to keep it that way. Maintaining your bedroom should be easy if you clean it like this regularly. A once-a-week cleaning should allow your bedroom to remain an appealing place to relax.

Maintenance of Bathroom

One of the most dreaded tasks to undertake within the household is the bathroom cleaning. Cleaning the bathroom doesn't have to be all that much work if it is done right. To get started, you should do a thorough cleaning of your bathroom. After this is done, all that will be necessary is regular upkeep and a good thorough cleaning once a month or so. Follow these simple steps to get you on your way to a cleaner bathroom. Have cleaners suited to clean the bathroom on hand and nearby.

Follow these tips for bathroom cleaning:

- Start by cleaning up all the laundry in the bathroom. This would include dirty towels, clothes, and rugs.

- Wash rugs in washer and let air dry, same for the shower curtain.

- Clean counter tops and any mirrors next. Using a cleaner for mirrors works best to avoid streaking.

- Use an antibacterial cleaner for your countertops.

- Clean the sink or sinks with antibacterial cleaner as well. This will insure that you rid the area of any bacteria that may be lingering. Shine the chrome of the faucets with a soft rag.

- Clean the toilet next. Take bleach or pine oil and pour a cup or two into the basin of the toilet, let sit for a few minutes.

  Work your way down, cleaning the lid, the seat, under the seat, and around the outside of the toilet. After you are finished with that, take your toilet brush and scrub in and around the basin to clean. Flush.

- Cleaning the bathtub depends on how dirty it is, spray a heavy-duty cleanser and let sit for a while. Go back and scrub until the residue, whether it is mildew, soap scum, or just dirt, until it comes clean.

- Wipe down walls and cabinets with a damp sponge and don't forget the door handles. It is a good idea to give the whole bathroom a once over with a disinfectant spray to kill any last germs.

- Lastly, mop the floor. When it dries and your rugs are dry as well, you can lie them back down.

- Don't forget to replace the toilet paper roll and keep a stock under the counter.

Maintenance of Kitchen

Cleaning up the kitchen is part of good house-keeping. Not only is it easier to cook and bake in a clean kitchen, but clean surfaces and storage containers will keep your family healthier and safer.

Follow these easy tips and make the kitchen automatically cleaner and less cluttered. Make cleaning second nature and you'll save time and money.

- Have a place for everything. It's much easier to use a utensil or appliance, clean it and put it away when it has a home.

- Don't mix ammonia and bleach because it will create toxic fumes.

- Identify spots in your kitchen that accumulate clutter and take a few minutes everyday to clear those spots and place objects in their correct homes.

- Try to end each day with a clean, empty kitchen sink. Run the dishwasher before you go to bed and unload it first thing in the morning.

- A sponge is actually a great way to spread germs.

Making Cleaning Solutions at Home

- For window washing solution, mix 1/3 cup vinegar and 1/4 cup rubbing alcohol in a 1 quart spray bottle. Fill up with water.

- Dry baking soda cleans chrome perfectly.

- Cream of tartar and water mixed to a paste will clean porcelain.

- A paste of baking soda and water will clean coffee stains.

- Plain liquid Ivory soap mixed with water is one of the best all-purpose cleaners. You can keep this solution in a spray bottle, but only use a bit of soap or the mixture may become too foamy to spray.

- Use a cut lemon half sprinkled with salt to clean copper.

- Dissolve 1/4 cup baking soda in 1 quart of warm water for a good general cleaner.

Preventions

- Clean up spills as they occur so you won't be faced with one huge cleaning session.

- Any tool or appliance which doesn't get used during a week of cooking should be cleaned and stored to save counter and cupboard space and cleaning time.

- It's easier to clean a grill if you do it after each use. Also oil the grill rack before each use to make cleanup easier.

- Wash as you go. Fill one half of a double sink or a separate waterproof tub with hot soapy water and drop in utensils as you use them. Food won't dry on the utensils and cleanup will be a breeze.

- Once every 7-10 days, remove all the food from your refrigerator, wipe down the inside with warm soapy water, clean all the shelves and trays, then replace the food.

- Place an open box of baking soda in the back of the fridge.

- Once a month, remove all the food from your pantry, wipe down with a clean damp cloth, check for spoilage and expiration dates, then replace items in their designated places.

Maintenance of Stainless Steel

Stainless steel is known for its ability to be a clean surface that resists corrosion and rust. Dirt, dust and grime, however, put stainless steel at risk for corrosion and rust.

Water and a Cloth

Routine cleaning can be accomplished by using warm water and a cloth. This is the least risky option for cleaning stainless steel. Dry with a towel or cloth to prevent water spots. Wipe in the directions of the polish lines.

Mild Detergent, (dish washing liquid) and Cloth

For cleaning that needs more power, mild detergent and warm water can do a great job without damaging the stainless steel. Make sure you rinse the surface thoroughly to prevent staining and spotting.

Glass Cleaner for Fingerprints

Fingerprints are one of the biggest complaints about stainless steel, but can be taken care by using glass cleaner or household ammonia. Rinse thoroughly and towel dry.

Stainless Steel Mistakes

- Do not use abrasive cleaners that will scratch the surface.
- Do not forget to rinse.
- Do not use cleaners containing chlorine.
- Do not use steel wool or steel brushes.
- Do not assume it's the cleaner.

How to Do Laundry Efficiently?

Doing laundry efficiently is another way to show your capability of smart house-keeping works. Some of the tips for efficiently handling the house laundry are as follows:

- Sort your laundry. Separate jeans from the rest of the clothing and then sort by colour.

- Further sort by removing delicate items like silks and sweaters from tougher things like towels or sweatshirts.

- Check the labels of each clothing item to determine if it's machine washable or if it needs to be dry-cleaned or hand-washed.

- Turn sweaters and black clothing inside out. That way,

any snags on the sweaters are on the inside. Turning black clothing inside out helps slow fading.

- Use garment bags for delicate clothing and for sweaters. It protects them from damage during the wash cycle.

- Go through the pockets of all of the clothes as you're sorting.

   Check shirt and jacket pockets as well as pants pockets and remove anything you find.

- Remember that a stray pen, marker or crayon could destroy an entire load of clothing.

- Wash your laundry on cold water using soap made for cold-water washing. It's more efficient and wears your clothing less.

- Fill the wash machine no more than 2/3 of the way full and don't push the clothes down. Place them in the machine and let them fall in naturally. If you pack the wash machine too tightly, your clothes won't come clean.

- Add the recommended amount of soap and turn the machine on to the cycle that matches the clothing inside.

- Wash your white laundry last. Fill the machine with water before adding the clothing. Put in a small amount of bleach and let it agitate to mix well before you put the clothes in the machine.

- Dry your clothes immediately to avoid mildew. Leave the clothes in the dryer only as long as it takes for them to dry. Remove and fold them or hang them up immediately for best results.

Folding Laundry Efficiently

- Be sure you have a very handy flat surface, such as the top of your washer and dryer or if you are very lucky a long counter. Use the dust cloth to wipe away any lint or dust that might be there.

- Start your folding as soon as the dryer is done! It's better to have the clothes slightly damp than over dry. If you are hanging your clothes to dry, try to fold them as soon as you take them off the line, right into the laundry basket if you have no table or counter to work on.

- As you pull each item out of the dryer or off the line, fold it carefully and make neat stacks of: shirts, t-shirts, pants, underwear, towels etc.

- If the clothes belong to more than one person, you could make a stack for each person instead of by item type. Having them in groups makes putting them away easier.

- Even if you plan to hang some items on hangers, it's still better to fold them neatly until they get to the hangers, than to leave them in a crumpled pile. They will be much less wrinkled this way.

- By folding the clothes as soon as they are dry and not leaving them to cool in a tangled heap in the dryer, they are much less wrinkled and much easier to iron. Many things don't even need to be ironed if taken out and folded or put on hangers right away.

Maintenance of Electronic Devices

One of the biggest enemies to your electronics is dust. Dust settles, thickens, and can eventually block important components like fans. A nonworking fan leads to overheated and possibly ruined electronics.

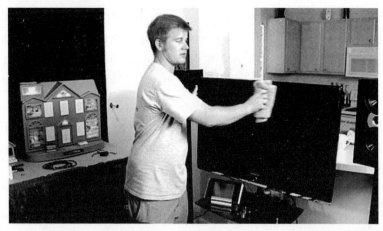

No matter what kind of duster you are using, the main point is that you dust your electronics and dust often. You may think dusting is a hassle, but try replacing a computer that had its fan blocked by dust.

In case you have not noticed, television and computer screens are magnets for dust and dirt. A screen can get dusty and grimy or be covered with fingerprints. Different types of screens will require different cleaning solutions, so be sure to check the manufacturer's instructions.

Never spray cleaner directly onto a screen because, you will inevitably spray too much and have it dripping into your electronics. Instead spray a small amount onto your cleaning cloth and then wipe the screen working in a circular motion. Do not use paper towels on your screens, they can scratch and pit the surface. Instead choose a soft cleaning cloth.

For many types of screens ammonia free glass cleaner or isopropyl alcohol can do a great job of cleaning without damaging the screen. These can be a great alternative to the sometimes expensive commercial screen cleaners. Always test in a small area to be sure.

Further, never allow any type of food or drink near your electronic equipment, but spills still happen. If a spill happens near electronics, one of the first things to do is to try to minimize the damage, turn off and unplug the electronic devices.

Try to wipe up as much of the spill as possible and keep it from spreading. Once you have gotten up as much as you can, it is time to assess the damage.

If the spill was on the surface and did not make it inside your electronic device, count yourself lucky and be more cautious in the future.

If a small amount seeped into the electronics, you may be able to let it dry out, or to remove the cover pieces and wipe up the inside. Use extreme caution when trying to do this yourself, and be aware that many warranties are voided if you remove cover pieces from electronic devices.

Cotton swabs dipped in isopropyl alcohol can be great for cleaning keyboards and push button devices that have been spilled on.

Quick Tips for Cleaning a DVD Player

DVD players attract as much or more dust as the other electronics in our home. Be sure to dust with a micro fibre cloth or electrostatic duster at least weekly, to keep your model running smoothly.

The insides of a DVD player can get dirty and dusty too. A great tool is a DVD disc cleaner. This cleaner looks just like a disc with some extra little brushes on its surface. Some DVD cleaner kits even come with supplies to clean and modify scratches on your discs.

Quick Tips for Cleaning a Cell Phone

Cell phones during a typical week will only need a quick wipe down with a dry cloth, or with a baby wipe. If a spill happens, turn off your phone, take out the battery, and use a soft cleaning cloth with a little isopropyl alcohol as your first line of defense. For sticky spills that stick in crevices, turn off your phone, and try a cotton swab dipped in isopropyl alcohol rubbed around the button surfaces and crevices.

Quick Tips for Cleaning MP3 Players

MP3 players, need to be wiped down as well. Refer to manufacturers instructions for the particular model. Remember that MP3 players with screens need special care. Do not use paper towels as they may scratch the surface. Instead, use a clean, soft, dry cloth. For more intense cleaning, try an ammonia free glass cleaner on the same type of cloth. Ear buds and cords may need to be wiped down as well.

If your MP3 player has been spilled on, it may need a cotton swab dipped in cleaner to get dirt out of the crevices. There are some commercially available scratch restoration kits that will minimize scratches.

■ ■ ■

CHAPTER 5

Household Budget

Household budgets are the most important part of good house-keeping jobs. The budgets allow us to make proper arrangements at home, as without any budget a house cannot run smoothly. While everyone has a budget, some people have better budgets than others.

Here are some quick tips for managing households' budgets:

Make Goals

Goals can be as short-term or as long-term as going on vacation next spring. Start small and be realistic about what you want to accomplish. Make your goals personal. Decide what you want, not what someone wants for you.

Involve your Entire Household

Create a budget together, and explain to everyone that they

may be asked to make sacrifices. If you're not open and honest with the rest of the family, you run a risk of them sabotaging your budget by not adhering to it.

Budget in Fun

A budget that leaves no money for an occasional dinner at a nice restaurant or for a family outing at an amusement park is designed to fail. You have to pay yourself first. Your budget should help you, not put you in a bind.

Save, Save, Save

If you're not having luck saving the traditional way, change your mindset. Most people look at saving as putting away money for a rainy day. Saving is the solution of all the problems of rainy day.

Take Inventory

For a week, keep a record of how you spend your money. If you buy a cup of coffee, write it down. Then, go back and figure out ways to cut your weekly expenses. Sounds small, but over a year it will really add up.

Remember: Saving is Habit-Forming

A wise man once said, "A bad habit is easy to make but hard to live with. But a good habit is hard to make and easy to live with."

Expect Changes

Look down the road, and get into the habit of thinking ahead. If you know that your situation is going to change — a new baby, new clothes for winter, a new job — plan for it. If not, these things will catch up with you and blow your budget.

Get Rid of High-Interest Debt

Focus on identifying high interest-rate debt and work on paying that debt off. Check with the credit union of your job; many have lower percentage rate credit cards and loans. The best way to keep from spending too much on credit cards is to be open-minded about what you're spending.

Find A System that Works for You

It could be the envelope system, a bank or a credit union. If it works for you and your family, use it. Experts warn, however, that it will be harder for you to save if you keep your money where it is always available to you.

Remember: You have to Walk Before you Can Run

Creating and sticking to a budget that works won't be easy, but in the end it will help you make the most of your hard-earned money.

Why Have a Budget?

Keeping Track

There is only so much money from month-to-month. But the question remains where does it all go? A sizeable portion pays for housing, food and basic living. Another portion pays for transportation. But where does the rest go? Budgeting allows you to track your monthly expenditures so that you can plan key savings strategies for important short- and long-term goals.

Limits Spending

Having a financial budget may find that about 5-10% of your total spending may be for purchases that are not needed. What could you do with that extra 5-10%? Perhaps your future plans include buying your first home, going back to school, saving for your child's college, paying down debt or simply setting aside cash for a special trip. A budget will identify expenses that can be cut so that you can set goals on making important long-term savings.

Disciplining Yourself

Your goal is to rid yourself of instant gratification (the symptom of credit card use). The budget sets guidelines on what and when items can be purchased.

Setting Goals

Budgeting supports your financial goals and also good budgeting skills add these goals into the budget, which may include:

- saving for your first home
- paying down debt
- preparing for a new child
- planning for retirement

Prepare for Emergencies

The key benefit of a budget is that it helps prepare for emergencies with established expense reduction plans.

Budgeting is an integral part of society. In today's hurry up and get it done society; every day we are trying to budget our time, our meals, our kids' time and our money. Unfortunately for many, most of this process is done mentally and never put on paper. A written budget is simply a formal written summary of your goals and intentions in terms of money.

Budgeting requires you to look ahead and formalize future

goals. By establishing a budget, you can set goals for achieving a certain level of things and monitor your expenses.

Goals and budgeting are very much tied together. The closer you come to the goals you have set for yourself, the closer you will come to achieving the budget amount you need. You'll know you are on top of your house-keeping when you can tell yourself that you have saved enough for a vacation next year or a new car without having the members miss anything important.

How to Get Your Finances in Order?

It is all too easy to let your spending get out of control. Before you know it your bills will be more than you can comfortably handle and the pressure can build up fast. In order to have a quality life it is important to get your finances in order. A plan of action is needed if you are ever going to get your bills under control.

You should stop using charge cards if you are in financial trouble and get started on a home budget today. An emergency fund will sure help out when trouble comes your way. If things are so far gone you do not know where to start, you may want to consider getting professional help to get help get your financial life on the right path.

You may want to consider stopping any charge cards you now have until things get better. Most people spend more using credit cards than they will when paying cash. It is all too easy to think it is not due until next month. The trouble is next month always comes faster than you may realize. It may be hard to stop using your credit card but your future may depend upon it. To help you get your spending under control is essential to set up a home budget.

Setting up a home budget that you can live with should be on the top of your priority list. You must know how much money you have coming in and how much money is going out. Food and shelter should go at the top of your list, then go down the line and put all of your bills on your budget. Make choices you can stick with so down the road when life gets hard you can stay on track.

An emergency fund is the very best defense you can have when it comes to sticking to your budget.

Starting an emergency fund will do wonders for your future. No matter how careful you are, things are going to happen that cost a lot of money to fix. These problems can blow your budget out of the water if you are not properly prepared.

Start small and put back a little each week. Small amounts add up fast if you make starting an emergency fund a priority in your life.

Not having enough money to pay your bills can be very stressful. Sometimes seeking professional help may be the best answer. Check to see if your city may offer some type of free debt counselling. Search out the help you need.

Getting your finances in order will help you out in more ways than you may realize. Once the stress of not having enough money to make it is gone you can begin to live life to the fullest.

What Makes Up a Budget?

Income

The budget starts with how much money you bring home on a monthly basis. Income sources include:

- employment income

- alimony received

- investment income

- social security

- support payments

- savings

- your goal should be around 90-98% or less

- the remaining 2-10% of your income should be allocated for savings

Housing Expenses

Housing expenses will likely be your largest expense item, especially if you own a home. Housing expenses include:

- your mortgage payment with escrow (taxes, insurance)

- monthly rental payment if you do not own

- utility services (electric, gas, oil, water, garbage, etc.)

- telephone, internet, cable

- house repairs and maintenance

Transportation

Transportation expenses include:

- auto loan payments
- auto insurance
- fuel expenses
- maintenance and repairs
- taxes, licensing
- parking
- public transportation

Family or Personal Care

Family care expenses include:

- family care insurance (health, disability, life, dental, etc.)
- doctor, dental, eye care, hospital visits
- veterinarian expenses
- prescriptions and over-the-counter medications
- child care
- elder care
- health clubs

Living Expenses

Home living expenses include:

- food
- home living supplies
- school and work lunches
- snacks, vendors

- clothing
- education-related expenses
- home services (cleaning, gardening)
- postage and paper supplies

Family Recreation

Recreation expenses include:

- dining out
- movies out and rentals
- outside entertainment
- cigarettes, beer, wine, liquor
- birthdays and holidays
- vacation travel
- weekend, day trips
- gambling, lottery tickets

Obligations

Obligation expenses include:

- credit card payments
- student loan payments
- home equity line or loan payments
- personal loan payments
- alimony, child support payments
- judgment or liens
- other assessed taxes
- charitable donations

Savings

Savings include:

- PF contributions
- NSC contributions
- investments
- savings (personal, college, retirement)

10-steps Budget Guide

Someone has rightly said, "Budgets are for cutting, that's why you set them." A home budget should be used as a way to track spending versus income, so that one can do something more than just covering expenses from one month to the other. Here are 10 steps for creating an effective budget:

Use Excel

With an MS Excel sheet, your budget tracking would just get easier! There's not a more simple way to manage things than by using excel. And the good news for amateurs is that you don't have to know much about the program to make it effective. Create several columns and list your income and expenses. With a little effort, and maybe some help from the web, you'll be able to automatically total your budget figures, making things much easier on you!

On the other hand, if you don't have a computer or don't want to use it, get down with a pen and a notebook and start listing things.

Determine Monthly Net Income

It's simple… Start with noting down how much money you make on a monthly basis. Remember, though, the government would take a great chunk from it, you need to make sure you track your net income instead of your gross income.

What's the difference? Well, net income is the actual figure that goes into you bank when you cash your check; or, in other words, it's what you don't pay in taxes. Your gross figure would be what you would get paid if the government didn't take out their share. Make sure you figure your budget off of your net income.

Calculate your Fixed Costs

Consider your car payment, mortgage, health insurance, car insurance, and anything else that doesn't change month to month. Also, make sure you include in that set of expenses 10 to 15 percent of your income you'll be paying yourself with.

After all, if you don't plan on saving and treat it like a must, you'll never do it. Make your long term savings goals a real expense to you now.

Note Down your Variable Costs

These costs include the expenses that you can plan on from month to month but that can change depending on your behaviour or other priorities. Your groceries, eating out, entertainment, and clothing expenses could be on this particular list.

Since you have the capability of lowering these expenses based on your behaviour, you can use this as one of the biggest tools to cut into your debts and/or build wealth. You need to know your variable costs in order to make changes in your spending habits.

Set Goals

After determining all of your costs, you need to set goals. Pick numbers under each of your categories that reflect something to shoot for. This applies mostly to your variable costs, as you have the power each month to cut down where you need to.

Keep your Receipts

Keep a track of your receipts or else you'll forget to record some of your spending.

Nightly Recording

Just do it. Yeah… it's understandable that there are going to be times when this is the last thing you want to worry about after getting home from a long day at work. If you can keep up on it, you'll be glad. Nightly recordings eliminate a lot of the possibility of error, meaning you'll have a more accurate set of numbers at the end of the month to evaluate.

Label your Expenses

You should have several categories for your expenses. For example, you might have a health care category or an automobile category. Within each one, make sure you are recording specific expenses. That way when you see a large figure that month for your car, you'll be able to identify where changes need to be made.

Evaluate

After following your budget for a month or so, you'll want to see where you can improve. Find areas where you spend more than may be necessary. You may even find that you're allowing yourself too much in a particular area. Again, if your budget doesn't stretch you a little bit, neither will your money

Make a Leisure Fund

It may sound ridiculous, but it is absolutely essential! In other words, pay yourself some money to have fun with each month. Personal budgets get such a bad rap because most think there's no room for fun. Not so! Your budget should empower you! Give yourself a modest allowance to spend on yourself! It's fun!

■■■

CHAPTER 6

First Aid

It is very important that every home, and especially those with children, have a first aid kit on hand in case of accidental injuries. Appropriate members of the household should know where the kit 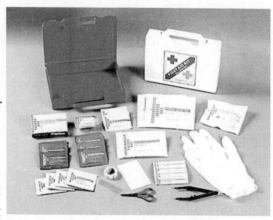 is kept and how to use each item.

For maintaining a home first aid kit, one must gather all items of the first aid from the local pharmacy. A first aid suggests choosing a container that is clean, roomy, durable, and easy to carry and simple to open-for instance, a tote bag. Medicines should be stored in their proper containers and properly marked with dosage and instructions on how and when to take them.

Almost everyone will need to use a first aid kit at some time. Take the time to prepare a kit to have available for home and travel. First aid kits may be basic or comprehensive. What you need depends on your medical training and how far you are from professional medical help. Ready-made first aid kits are commercially available from chain stores or outdoor retailers. However, you can make a simple and inexpensive first aid kit yourself.

Some of the important things to be included in the first aid kit are:

- The kit should include a list of the contents it contains.

- In addition, keep in the kit emergency phone numbers for the family physician and pediatrician.

- Include phone numbers for emergency services, such as the local police, fire department and ambulance service.

- Also, if family members have life-threatening allergies to food, medications or bee stings, include a list of allergies for each family member, as well as medications used by each person.

- Remember to store first aid kits in places that children cannot reach, but that are easily accessible for adult family members.

- Check the kit regularly to replace missing items and make sure that the items haven't passed their expiration dates.

Home and Travel First Aid Kits

Home first aid kits are usually used for treating these types of minor traumatic injuries:

- Burns

- Cuts
- Abrasions (scrapes)
- Stings
- Splinters
- Sprains
- Strains

First aid kits for travel need to be more comprehensive because a drug store may or may not be accessible. In addition to personal medical items, the kit should contain items to help alleviate the common symptoms of viral respiratory infections such as these:

- Fever
- Nasal congestion
- Cough
- Sore throat

It should also contain items to treat these ailments:

- Cuts
- Mild pain
- Gastrointestinal problems
- Skin problems
- Allergies

How to Make a First Aid Kit?

- Try to keep your first aid kit small and simple. Stock it with multi-use items. Almost anything that provides good visibility of contents can be used for a household first aid kit.

- If your kit will be on the move, a water-resistant, drop-proof container is best.

- Inexpensive nylon bags, personal kits, fanny packs, or make-up cases serve very well.

- You do not need to spend a lot of money on a fancy 'medical bag'. Use resealable sandwich or oven bags to group and compartmentalize items.

- Put wound supplies in one bag and medications in another.

What to Put in Home Kit?

- Acetaminophen, ibuprofen and aspirin tablets (Aspirin should not be used to relieve flu symptoms or be taken by children.)

- Cough Suppressant

- Antihistamine

- Decongestant tablets

- Oral medicine syringe (for children)

- Bandages of assorted sizes

- Bandage closures; safety pins

- Triangular bandage

- Elastic wraps

- Gauze and adhesive tapes

- Sharp scissors with rounded tips

- Antiseptic wipes

- Antibiotic ointment

- Hydrogen peroxide

- Disposable, instant-activating cold packs
- Tweezers

What to Put in a Travel Kit?

A travel first aid kit may contain these items:

- Adhesive tape
- 4" × 4" sterile gauze pads
- Antacid - For indigestion
- Antidiarrheal (Imodium, Pepto-Bismol, for example)
- Antihistamine cream
- Antiseptic agent (small bottle liquid soap) - For cleaning wounds and hands
- Aspirin - For mild pain, heart attack
- Adhesive bandages (all sizes)
- Diphenhydramine (Benadryl) - Oral antihistamine
- Book on first aid
- Cigarette lighter - To sterilize instruments and to be able to start a fire in the wilderness (to keep warm and to make smoke to signal for help, for examples)
- Cough medication
- Dental kit - For broken teeth, loss of crown or filling
- Exam gloves
- Small flashlight
- Ibuprofen (Advil is one brand name)
- Insect repellant
- Knife (small Swiss Army-type)

- Moleskin - To apply to blisters or hot spots
- Nasal spray decongestant - For nasal congestion from colds or allergies
- Nonadhesive wound pads (Telfa)
- Polysporin antibiotic ointment
- Oral decongestant
- Personal medications and items
- Phone card with at least 60 minutes of time (and not a close expiration date) plus at least 10 quarters for pay phones and a list of important people to reach in an emergency
- Plastic resealable bags (oven and sandwich)
- Pocket mask for CPR
- Safety pins (large and small)
- Scissors
- Sunscreen
- Thermometer
- Tweezers

How to Use a First Aid Kit?

Make sure you know how to properly use all of the items in your kit, especially the medications. Train others in your family to use the kit. You may be the one who needs first aid! Pack and use barrier items such as latex gloves to protect you from bodily fluids of others. Check the kit twice a year and replace expired medications. Find out the phone number of your regional poison control centre and keep the number with your kit.

Where to Keep the First Aid Kit?

- The best place to keep your first aid kit is in the kitchen. Most family activities take place here. The bathroom has too much humidity, which shortens the shelf life of items.

- The travel kit is for true trips away from home. Keep it in a suitcase or backpack or drybag, depending on the activity.

- A first aid kit for everyday use in the car should be just like the home first aid kit. For that matter, you could keep similar kits in your boat (inside a waterproof bag), travel trailer, mobile home, camper, cabin, vacation home, and wherever you spend time.

■ ■ ■

CHAPTER 7

Gardening

Gardening is one of the most important activities in keeping the house smart. It not only enriches the beauty of the home but also gives way to fulfil the hobby of gardening. Not much to say the greenery outside the home energizes the home energy thus providing a positive feeling to the family  members. Some of the basis tips for a better garden are described here in this section.

Before Starting a Garden

Like all major tasks, you need to plan for starting a garden. At this point, selection of plants is very important.

Selecting plants is one of the toughest gardening tasks, simply because there are so many to choose from. Choosing of plants can be based on the following:

- **Quality of Nursery:** Take in an overview of the plant department.

- **Foliage:** Evaluate the condition of your plants. Are the leaves green, shiny and lush?

- **Shape:** Consider the shape of the plants. Are they compact and full, with multiple stems? Would they fill your space or overcrowd it.

- **Insects & Disease:** Inspect closely for signs of insects or disease. Check both sides of the leaves and the potting soil. Signs can include blackened areas, holes, spots, mushy areas, stickiness and distortions.

- **Root System:** Don't neglect the roots. If a plant is pot bound and the roots are growing out of the bottom, the plant may be stressed and take time to recover. If there aren't many roots and the plant lifts out very easily, it was probably recently repotted and could use more time to become garden worthy.

- **Stem Damage:** If the plant has a thick or woody stem, make sure there are no cracks or scars. Even prior damage can weaken a plant.

- **Weeds:** Weeds in the pot are competing with the plant for nutrients. They also signal some neglect on the part of the nursery staff.

- **Root Ball:** When buying a balled-and-burlapped tree or shrub, the root ball should feel solid. If it appears broken, there's a good chance the roots have had a chance to dry out and the plant will suffer.

- **Buds & Flowers:** Plants in bud will transplant and thrive better than plants in flower.

Starting a Garden

A good place to begin a garden is with the soil. As the saying goes, "Feed the Soil and the Plants will take care of Themselves"

For flower gardens, choose a site close to the door or with a good view from a favourite window. Place your garden where you'll see and enjoy it often. This will also motivate you to garden more.

The front lawn of the home is the best site for starting a garden as the homeowners found an attractive, sunny spot to add some colour and curb appeal. No matter how busy they are, they can enjoy their garden everytime they pull into their driveway or look out their front window.

Garden Tools

The right tool makes any job easier and that is no exception in the garden. Gardeners collect many tools over the years, but there is always one tool that they absolutely couldn't garden without. If you are just starting out, there are a few basic tools that will get you  started. However, don't spend a fortune until you've had a chance to try a few and see what your preferences are.

Some of the basic garden tools are:

- **Shovels:** Garden shovels have round, pointed blades. They're absolutely necessary for moving soil, digging holes and planting. Look for one with a flat edge at the top of the blade. It provides a better surface for your foot. Here's a sampling of what to look for in garden shovels.

- **Trowels:** Most planting will require you get down on your knees with a trowel. Steel blades will last longest. Handle choice is a matter of personal preference. Soft rubber handles are easier on the grip. There are also ergonomic designs that take the stress off of your wrist. A narrow blade is good for digging in solid soil. Wide, rounded blades remove soil faster.

- **Pruners:** Pruning, deadheading and shaping plants goes on all year in the garden. Good pruners will not only make your job easier, it will make a cleaner cut on the plants and not tear or rip. Basically there are 2 types of pruners- anvil and bypass. Look for pruners with replaceable parts and blades that can be sharpened.

- **Hoes:** Weeds are a fact of gardening life. Hoes can make quick work of weeds. They can also be used to break up soil that isn't to compacted. For strength, look for a rolled steel blade that is riveted to the handle. Smaller blades allow you to get in between plants.

- **Garden forks:** Nothing works as well as a fork to break up soil. Garden forks are slightly shorter and thicker than pitch forks. The strongest have square, rather than flat tines. A garden fork can usually take the place of a spade, if it's the right type of fork.

- **Rakes:** Yard rakes will help you get fall's leaves out of your gardens and also collect all your garden debris. Tines with some spring can be used in the garden without too much damage to plants. A narrow rake can maneuver around plants easier, but a wide rake makes quicker work of leaves.

Heavy metal rake are long and straight with teeth about 3" long. They are necessary to smooth out newly tilled garden soil and break up clumps.

- **Wheelbarrows and Carts:** Toting things around the garden can really become a chore without the aid of a wheelbarrow or cart.

  Plants, soil and compost all have to get to your garden somehow. The size of your cart will depend on the size of your garden.

- **Water cans and Hose:** A good watering can will have a handle that balances in your hand. Handles that curve from the front of the can to the bottom make it easier to tilt.

  Again, large may seem better, but don't get a can that is so large you can lift it when full.

Some important tips for garden tools:

- Forged tools will cost more, but they are more durable.
- Long handles provide more leverage. Short handles provide ore control, but can be hard on the back.
- Use a steel brush to clean off tools after each use.
- Keep handles from drying by rubbing with linseed oil.
- Sharpen your tools before storing for the winter. Protect with a coat of oil, wax or petroleum jelly
- Check and tighten screws and fasteners often.

Maintenance of a Garden

There is always something to do in the garden. Some plants are more demanding than others, but garden maintenance is always needed all over the year. Here are a few maintenance tips for different months of the years.

January

- Get those plant and seed catalogues out and start planning next season's garden. Cut the branches off of your trees to use as mulch in the garden.

- Scout tree branches and limbs for signs of egg masses

February

- Keep tabs on houseplants. Make sure they are getting enough humidity. Check for pests.

- Cut branches of flowering shrubs to bring inside for forcing.

- Inspect hemlocks for overwintering.

March

- If you have non-stone fruit trees like grapes and

raspberries it is time to prune them. Start all-purpose spray regimen.

- Start slow growing and cool season seeds like onions, leeks, parsley, celery, broccoli, cauliflower, cabbage, eggplant and peppers.
- Begin removing mulch from around rose bushes.
- Begin horticultural oil applications where needed to control pests.

April

- Harden off and move cool season crops to the garden.
- Plant asparagus roots and onion sets.
- Apply pre-emergent crabgrass killer after forsythia bloom.
- Remove mulch from on top of flowers.
- Re-mulch beds as necessary.
- Remove tent caterpillars and webs.
- Begin monitoring for signs of disease.

May

- Once your last frost data has passed, warm season crops can be planted.
- Start seeds for melon and squash. Hold until the end of may, to avert squash bugs and borers.
- Begin pinching annuals and perennials to make the plants fill in and produce more blooms.
- Prune evergreens when the new growth starts to turn a darker shade of green.
- Prune stone fruits (cherry, almond, peach, nectarine, plum) at bloom time.

- Stake tall perennials.
- Remove and dispose of azalea leaf gals before they turn white and release their spores.

June

- Prune flowering shrubs after the flowers begin to fade.
- Continue pinching flowers until first week of July.
- Deadhead and remove fading leaves from spring bloomers.
- Divide and transplant perennials.
- Take softwood cuttings from trees and shrubs to propagate new plants.
- Remove fallen fruits from below trees to prevent insect egg laying.
- Place red sticky sphere traps in apple trees to control apple maggot flies.
- Check undersides of rose leaves for rose slugs.
- Watch for scale infestations on Euonymus and pachysandra.
- Move houseplants outside.

July

- Stop pinching back flowers.
- Divide oriental poppies and iris.
- Keep deadheading.
- Remove leaves infested by miners, to control spread.
- Succession plant beans, lettuce, radishes and corn.
- Water newly planted trees and plants as necessary.

- Start seeds of fall crops like: broccoli, cabbage and cauliflower.

August

- Seed a fall crop of peas.
- Gather herbs and flowers for drying.
- Keep deadheading and harvesting.
- Begin taking cuttings for new plants.
- Sit and enjoy your garden in all its summer glory.

September

- Start moving houseplants indoors. Check for pests first.
- Seed a fall spinach crop.
- Seed cover crops on bare spots in the vegetable garden.
- Plant new trees and shrubs, to give them at least 6 weeks before frost.
- Plant spring flowering bulbs.
- Begin 'dark treatments' with your saved Poinsettia plant.
- Dry and store gladioli corms before a frost.

October

- Plant garlic and shallots.
- Have your soil tested and amend as needed.
- Harvest Brussel sprouts after a hard frost.
- Clean up garden debris. Remove all vegetable plants and fallen fruit.
- Remove dead annuals from the garden, after a frost.

- Cut back perennial foliage to discourage overwintering pests. Leave flowers with seeds for the birds.
- Start raking and composting leaves.

November

- Finish amending the soil.
- Cover exposed garden soil with a layer of shredded leaves, for the winter.
- Wrap screening around fruit tree trunks often damaged by mice and voles.
- Keep watering until the ground temperature reaches 40°F.
- Buy bulbs for winter forcing.
- Mulch rose bushes.

December

- Harvest any remaining root crops.
- Start rotating houseplants so they get equal light on all sides.
- Check stored corms and tubers for rot or dryness.
- Start paperwhites and amaryllis for winter blooms.

Garden Design

Good garden design starts with thinking about what you want. It's too late to plan your garden when you are standing in the nursery eyeing every new plant that tempts you.

Spend some time looking at your garden site, either during the off season, when you can really view it objectively or during the growing season, when your successes and failures make themselves known.

Purpose

The very first garden design consideration should be 'What do you want to use your garden for?' Aesthetic beauty is a given, unless it is a weed demonstration garden. But there are also other garden functions:

- Privacy from a busy street or neighbours.

- Space for small children to be comfortable.

- Own private space.

- Attract more birds and butterflies into the yard.

- Create a view from inside the house.

Style

You know what you want to use your garden for, what you are working with and how many resources you can devote to it. The style of the garden will reflect the different ideas. Some of the styles of the garden include:

- Formal or informal

- Four Season Interest

- Complement with house

- Flow with the natural landscape

Plant Selection

Each step should get easier and more fun. Plant selection should be one of the last things you consider, or you may be overwhelmed trying to create a design to accommodate the dozens (or hundreds or even thousands) of plants you crave.

- Keep in mind what the garden will be used for and when.

- Planting spring bulbs and early bloomers wouldn't be the wisest investment.

- In summer, look for lower maintenance of plants that don't require constant deadheading and staking to look good.

- For small children, choose plants that will bloom at their eye level, with interesting textures and scents and non-poisonous flowers and seeds.

- Make a list of the plants you like and group them by colour, texture and form, the garden design triumvirate. Also chart them by season of bloom and/or interest.

- Consider both flowers and foliage. There are more and more plants being bred with colourful foliage that will provide interest in the garden all season.

- Be sure to include some large anchor plants that will look good all year. These are usually shrubs and often evergreens.

Great Container Gardens

One can grow almost anything in a container. A simple potted basil plant could be considered a container garden, but there are so many other possibilities. Gardening in pots and

containers gives the ability to insure great soil, experiment with colour, move your garden with the sun and raise the garden to a comfortable working height.

Maybe the best feature of container gardening is the ability to create a whole new garden every time. Here are some tips :

Establish the Size of Container Garden

Make sure there is enough room in the container for the plants and soil. Take into account the mature size of the plants and their growing habits. Upright growers will need a wide base for balance. Sprawlers will need a pot deep enough to drape over.

As the plants grow, the root systems will fill the pot and the soil will dry more quickly. It's OK to fill the diameter of the container with plants, but make sure there is plenty of room for the roots to move downward into soil.

Provide Good Drainage

Always have drainage holes or at the very least, a 1-2 inch layer of gravel at the bottom of the container. If you are using a decorative pot without drainage holes, consider planting in a plastic pot with holes that is one size smaller than the decorative pot and using the plastic pot as an insert.

Soil Requirements for Container Gardens

Use a good potting soil mix, not garden soil. A mix with peat, perlite or vermiculite will retain moisture longer and yet be well draining. It will also be lighter and won't compact as the season goes on. Using a chunky-style potting mix in container of 5 or more gallons will help the soil mix remain loose even longer.

Choose Plants with Similar Cultural Requirements

In a garden bed, you can select which plants need water and which to pass over. Not so with a container garden. Select plants that will be happy with the same amounts of water, sun, heat and food. Avoid aggressive spreaders that will compete with neighbouring plants and consider dwarf varieties.

Favour Drought Tolerant Plants

Most container gardens are going to require daily watering in hot weather. Even so, there will be times when you potted plants are going to be baking in the sun.

Give your container a fighting chance by favouring plants that can handle the intensified heat and dry soil of a container garden.

Balance the Size of Plants and Container

Container gardens look best when the plants are in balance with the container. Try to make sure your tallest plants are not be more than twice the height of the container and that the fullness of the plant material is not more than half the width again as wide.

Judge Sun Exposure

Try not to site containers in full mid-day sun. Some plants require full sun, but container gardens heat up much more quickly and intensely than in the ground gardens. Most plants will welcome some relief from mid-day sun.

On the other hand, when you must position a container in the shade, consider putting it by a wall that can reflect some light back. The plants won't suffer from the extreme heat, but they will benefit from indirect light.

Watering Container Gardens

Lack of water can quickly kill plants in a container garden. Unlike plants grown in the ground, container plant roots can't move down deeply in search of subsurface water.

Check your containers daily for water needs. Check twice daily in the heat of summer and with smaller containers.

Fertilizing Container Gardens

Some potting mixes come with fertilizer already mixed in. Some don't. Either way, container plant roots can't spread out looking for additional food in the soil nearby, so you will need to replenish soil nutrients regularly. Good choices are a time released fertilizer mixed in when planting or a water soluble fertilizer every 2-4 weeks.

Keeping Container Gardens Fresh

Don't be afraid to switch out plant material for the change of season. No plant can go on blooming for ever. When one plant starts to fade, look for another to take its place. This way you can start your container garden in the spring and go until frost. With container gardens, sequence of bloom is entirely within the gardener's control.

■ ■ ■

CHAPTER 8

Interpersonal Relationships

What is Interpersonal Relationship?

To understand what a relationship is, how to bring one about, how to enhance one, and why relationships are diminished and lost, one must understand the power of a person's needs. The most important things in the world, to us, are the things we believe that we need. Needs affect opinions, attitudes, and viewpoints. Generally we're more aware of unfulfilled needs than the ones that are consistently met. Fundamental life needs in particular are so commonly accepted that we usually overlook them.

No one is aware of the air breathed, the ground walked on, the water drunk, and yet these are the needs we miss most when gone.

The key to good interpersonal relationships is simple once you understand the role that needs play in making a relationship weak, moderate, average, or strong. Let's give the word relationship a different definition from the dictionaries, for unlocking the meaning of the word often leads to greater understanding.

When two people have strong needs and each fills the other's needs, there is a powerful interpersonal relationship. When two people have weak needs and each fills the other's needs, there is a mild relationship.

When either person has strong needs and those needs are not being filled, there is a poor relationship. When either has weak needs and those needs are not being filled, there is a mild relationship, but one leaning more to the negative side than the positive.

When a weak need is not being filled, there isn't much caring either way.

To enhance any relationship is simple- find out what the other person needs and then fill that need. To end a relationship the reverse is true. Find out what the other person needs and keep those needs unfilled. It's as simple as that. The great principle of correspondence states, "As above, so below, as below, so above."

When you know the key to happiness you have also

learned the key to unhappiness. Without realising it, when you know how to be a failure, you also know how to be a success.

When you are successful at failing in interpersonal relationships, you also know how to be successful at succeeding in relationships, once the concept is understood. An individual who fails at a relationship is a person who neglects the needs of the partner.

So, it would follow that the first step to a successful relationship is to determine what needs the other person has. It is also vital to understand your own needs so that you can help the other person in the relationship to fill your needs.

Unfortunately, not only do the great majority of people fail to see or to understand the other person's needs, they do not understand their own. Children have wonderful relationships with their parents as long as their great needs are being filled.

When the needs are unfulfilled, the relationship changes and problems arise. As the child grows, needs change; it is essential that the parent recognise the changes. As it is with the child to the parent, so it is with the parent to the child.

The way to recognise needs in other people is by their response to you. When you do or say something and you get a positive response, you are well on the way to need recognition. As it is in others, so it is in you. What is it you respond to in a positive manner? What do you feel good about getting and about doing?

What are you totally guiltless about? What can you do with complete confidence and fearlessness? What emotional scene can you manipulate without fear or guilt? Look in these areas for your needs and you will in all probability find your answers.

When using our methods for need recognition and relationship enhancement, the land of alpha will open you to a good deal more information than a simple thoughtful moment at the Beta level of consciousness. Remember, our own needs are often hidden by fear, guilt, and past programming.

Relationship with Spouse

A healthy interpersonal relationship with spouse is very important. Women today are becoming so busy in their household or office work that they have no time for their spouse. Same with the husband, as they are too much busy in their  professional life. To make house a home, it is important to have a balanced relationship with the spouse, thus taking the credit of a good house keeper, which is not only beautifully decorated outside, but also is also beautiful internally.

Here are some of the tips which help to increase the many rewards that is possible in such a marvelous and complex relationship. For running a smooth and successful marriage one should draw attention on the following:

Do Not Hold Unrealistic Expectations

Before marriage, people often have unrealistic ideas about their spouse-to-be, expecting perfection in all aspects. This rarely, if ever, plays out in reality and can lead to unnecessary problems and concerns. By turning the table and expecting imperfection, Remember, you will be pleasantly surprised and pleased when your spouse is much more than you ever hoped for. This, in turn, will lead to contentment within the marriage.

Emphasise the Best in your Spouse

Since no one is endowed with all of the best qualities, emphasis should be placed on the positive qualities that a spouse possesses. Encouragement, praise, and gratitude should be expressed on a regular basis, which will strengthen these qualities and be beneficial in developing others. An attempt should be made to overlook or ignore negative characteristics.

Be your Mate's Best Friend

Try to think of what a best friend means and be one to your spouse. This may mean sharing interests, experiences, dreams, failures and upsets. It may involve understanding a spouse's likes and dislikes and attempting to please him or her in any way possible.

A best friend is also usually someone that can be confided to trusted, and relied upon. A spouse should be the kind of friend that one would want to keep throughout life.

Spend Quality Time Together

It is not enough to share meals, chores and small talk together. Spouses should also find time to focus on strengthening the relationship.

Often couples get busy with their own separate tasks and forget about working on one of the most important elements in life. Quality time may be anything from having a quiet, profound conversation to going for a nice long nature walk, to sharing a special hobby or project. Both spouses should enjoy the particular option chosen and distractions should be kept to a minimum.

Express Feelings Often

This is probably a very 'Western' concept and one that some people may have difficulty fulfilling, but it is important to be open and honest about one's feelings, both positive and negative. The lines of communication should always be open and any concerns should be brought to the attention of the other spouse as soon as they arise. The rationale of this is that what begins as a simple concern may grow into a major problem if it is not addressed quickly and properly. The 'silent treatment' has never been the remedy for anything.

Admit to Mistakes and ask for Forgiveness

The stronger person is the one who can admit when he or she is wrong, request pardon from the other, and work hard to improve his/her aspects that are in need of change. When a person is unwilling to do this, there will be little growth and development in the marriage.

Never Bring up Mistakes of the Past

It can be very hurting for another person to be reminded of past mistakes. One may remember errors that were made so that they are not repeated, but this should not be done excessively.

Certainly, as humans, we are not in the position to judge another person. Advice may be given, but not in a harmful manner.

Surprise Each Other at Times

This may entail bringing home a small gift or flowers,

preparing a special meal, dressing up and beautifying oneself (this is not only for women), or sending a secret note in a lunchbox. A little imagination will go a long way here. The idea is to spice up the marriage and avoid getting into a dull routine that may negatively affect the marriage.

Have a Sense of Humour

This particular aspect can go a long way in preventing arguments and brightening the atmosphere of the home. Life is a constant stream of challenges and tests, and to approach it in a light-hearted manner will help to make the journey smoother and more enjoyable.

You may also find that your spouse enjoys this characteristic and looks forward to spending time with you because of it.

Quick Tips for Discussions and Disagreements

- Begin with the intention to resolve the issue. If both spouses have this intention and plan to consult together, it is more likely that there will be a successful resolution.

- Remember that it takes two to quarrel. If only one person chooses not to argue, there will be no argument. Generally, the one who is wrong does most of the talking.

- Both spouses should not be angry at the same time. If one of the spouses becomes upset, it is best if the other tries to remain calm and collected.

- Never yell at each other unless the house is on fire. Of course, house fires do not occur very frequently; yelling should occur at about the same rate.

112 Smart House-Keeping for Modern Women

- Never go to sleep with an argument unsettled. This is one of the worst things that can happen in a marriage and should be avoided as much as possible. This allows hurt feelings and thoughts to linger and generally exacerbates the problem.

- If one spouse needs to win, let it be your mate. Do not focus on winning yourself; this is the main reason that discussions tend to become heated.

Handling Teenagers

As a parent, having a child reach the teenage years is joyful as well as a situation that brings with it new and interesting child discipline challenges. Your child has now completed childhood and made it to young adulthood.

This breeds its own set of child discipline and child behavioural problems. You feel like it was just yesterday when your teenager begged you to take him out for ice cream, and asked for your help in one of the many small but precious moments of life.

Not only is your child now speaking an entirely new language, he/she no longer wants you around or even needs you to be around. You feel like you have been shunted out of his life unceremoniously; you are no longer his 'idol', you are more of a thorn in his side and for no fault of yours. Do not despair, all is not lost!

This is a typical teenage behaviour, and is a plea for independence, and it is up to you to find ways and means for the bond between your child and you to remain as strong as it ever was.

Some of the tips in handling a teenaged child are:

- Don't start off any conversation with your teen on a defensive note. You will only put them on the defensive, and it will get you nowhere.

- Even if you do have to address a controversial topic, start off on a positive and neutral note, and get them to start talking before the conversation escalates into an argument and thereafter into an open spat. If you only talk to them negatively, remember, they will not want to talk to you at all.

- Another important tip that will help you bond with your teen is to remember that are no longer child; he or she is now an independent young man or woman, who can think for themselves.

- Respect their wishes when they say they do not wish to talk now, and also respect their privacy: they will respect you for it at a later time.

- Make efforts to learn what your teen enjoys doing at this stage in life, and try to be more of a friend to them than a parent.

- Home is haven. Keep your home a safe haven for your teen, where you can renew your bonds with them.

- Make mealtimes a time for togetherness: this is the place where there is no peer pressure, and your teen will not feel embarrassed to be caught doing things for mom and dad.

- Bond with your teenager! Follow these tips and bond better with your teen so that your bond remains as strong and unshakeable as ever as both of you progress through life.

- With patience and constant effort, it is indeed possible to teach your teen not to argue and talk back at you.

- A sure-fire way of inviting problems into your relationship with your teenager is by sending mixed or unclear messages.

  Clear communication is an absolute must if you want to have a bonding relationship with your teenager.

- It helps build a foundation of trust, fosters a healthy self-esteem, encourages positive behaviour, and helps tone down frustration and stress in the family.

While many parents feel it is close to impossible to have a conversation with their teenager, there are ways. Your child really isn't becoming a new special breed of alien. They're just growing up and they still do want to connect with you. Try these tips to get, and keep, the conversation rolling in your home:

- Use your active listening skills and watch out for those door slammers.

- Talk often with your teen to bring out positive opinions, ideas, and behaviours by using an affirmative tone and body language.

- Treat your teenager with the same respect you would have them treat you. Say, 'hi', 'I love you', 'how was your day', etc.

- Your tone of voice is extremely important. Yelling simply doesn't work.

- The loud noise will shut down the listener (your teen) and you will not get through. If you feel the need to yell, 'time out' of the conversation until you have better control.

- Be precise and detailed about what you expect. Write it down and use an action plan if you feel there is a need.

- If you're giving your teenager instructions, write them down. It's a fail-safe may for teens and adults.

  This way they will remember what they are expected to do and you can feel sure that you 'told' them correctly. Remember, to-do lists will keep you stress free.

- Do things together one-on-one and with the whole family. Good times often bring about great conversations, and wonderful memories.

- 'Do as I say, not as I do' doesn't work. Modelling is the best way of learning. You are your teenager's model and they will emulate your behaviours.

- Never shut your teen out to show that you disapprove of their behaviour. If you need time before you can talk to them about something that has upset you, tell them that you need time. Don't walk away silently.

- 'Because I said so' actually works when you are being pulled into a power struggle in discipline situations.

- You are the parent, and because of this, you do have the

final say. Teenagers know this and trust you because of it. But do try to explain your reasoning whenever possible.

Helping Children in their Exam Time

How to Help your Children Survive Exam Nerves?

Examinations are important milestones in your children's school life. Younger children need much more assistance than older children in preparing for exams. The guidance that you provide in the early stages will enable your children to study with discipline and dedication later on, on their own. If your children are still in kindergarten or primary classes, you will need to invest much more time.

However, with older children, you may face problems of a different kind—disobedience and rebellion, which require greater tact. Examinations are a menace only for the unprepared. Be moderately strict with your children—they'll thank you for it when they come out with flying colours.

Some of the tips in helping out the children from their anxieties include:

- Never let your children postpone studying until a day

before the exams. This will only increase their anxiety and stress levels.

- Preparation is the key to success. Don't listen to any excuses and don't be swayed by assurances.

- The best course is to have your children study for some time everyday.

  Even if this is not possible, ensure that they begin preparing for the exams at least two to three weeks in advance.

- Do not impose yourself on your children. Some children require more support while others are happier studying on their own.

  However, let them know that you're always there to help them.

- It is not enough to read up matter. Your children should be able to recall the same in the examination hall.

- Hold question and answer sessions where you ask them random questions on the subject once they have finished studying.

- Prepare a timetable for each child. You can cover subjects in the order of the examination schedule or you can tackle difficult subjects first. For younger children, two to three hours of study a day should suffice.

- Children in the secondary and higher secondary classes should study for four or five hours a day when the exams are due.

  Alternate languages and practical subjects like mathematics to minimize boredom.

- Especially for older children, access to question papers

from previous years is a must. These may be available in the school library, with teachers or you can secure them from the senior students.

- Have them solve at least one or two papers in each subject, within the given time limit. This is like a rehearsal and helps in mitigating exam nerves.

  It will also give your child an idea of how much time to allot for each question.

- Don't allow your children to stay up or wake up too early. Make sure that they get at least eight hours of sleep.

- Inadequate sleep affects the brain's functioning and will reduce your children's retention. Discourage use of caffeine or other stimulants to remain awake.

- Children these days suffer from as much stress as adults. Do not pressurise your child ever.

- Do not entertain negativity and empower them with confidence if they start moaning about previous performances.

- Create a study-ritual for your children. Encourage them to use the same place to study everyday, preferably somewhere quiet and pleasant.

- The outdoors is a great option as well. Let them be silent and make a resolve to study well before beginning the session. End every session with a revision of what has been covered.

- Set small goals—one or two chapters or even topics. If they are studying for long durations, schedule breaks every one or two hours.

  Let them do what they like, such as go for a walk, meditate or solve a puzzle.

- Older children may benefit from group study, especially for subjects that they find difficult.

- It is preferable if your child can go to his friends' houses rather than having them over. This way, he can leave if the session is proving to be a waste of time.

- On the D-Day, wake your children up well in time and serve them a light breakfast. Set aside time for a disciplined revision.

- Ensure that they have their pens and pencils, examination pad and other necessary items before leaving the house.

■ ■ ■

CHAPTER 9

Making a Happy Home

Power of Positive Thinking

The 'mind' is an important resource that displays the ability to generate a desired outcome. The power of positive thinking manifests in success and subsequently raised level of confidence.

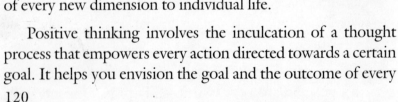

Positive thinking refers to an optimistic approach that adds quality to every choice that manifests, within every situation. Human desire changes with the acquisition of every new dimension to individual life.

Positive thinking involves the inculcation of a thought process that empowers every action directed towards a certain goal. It helps you envision the goal and the outcome of every subsequent action. The route map towards achievement is defined by the 'power' of positive thinking

Stories of the awkward, child off the streets becoming a business tycoon or the plain, freckled face making it to the celluloid charts are invariably credited to the power of positive thinking. The process of positive thinking involves:

- Meditating on the desired goal.

- Developing an action plan.

- Developing a clear image of the goal, in the 'accomplished' form.

- Brainstorming to enhance the ability to visualize.

- Empowering every subsequent real-time action with self-discipline and patience.

- Positive affirmation within the subconscious mind, to reflect in behaviour and action.

- Routing all pursuits and daily interactions towards the achievement of the goal.

These seven steps towards realization of our aspirations stand on the platform of transference. The power generated by thought is automatically transferred to every subsequent action. The 'imagine' and 'action plan' game has a ripple effect. The more vivid the imagination and brainstorming, the closer you are towards the realization of your dreams.

Positive thinking transmits thoughts and empowers associated people and actions. Thus charged with enthusiasm, you are able to foster courage and attempt the otherwise unimaginable.

Positive thinking is an ongoing confirmation of your personal belief in your own words and actions. It generates a 'midas touch' kind of effect, and persuades others in the peripheral to invest in your plans and give into the enthusiasm you display. It is in this space that the power of positive thinking manifests in the form of effective goal setting.

The rejection of doubt, increased level of concentration, show of grit and determination and mind-control are the major tools that tweak every interaction towards the realization of your desire.

Self-motivation to charge towards the light at the end of the tunnel comes from mental manifestation of the advantages and benefits of your aspiration. You need to make the images larger than life. When all mental energy is poured into the single mold, day after day, the design sets and affects your attitude and actions. The raised level of confidence is clearly noticed by others around and the result is that they begin to generate opportunities.

Corresponding situations automatically manifest turning thought into reality. The power of positive thinking enables you to develop the right mental attitude, conductive to growth.

There are a number of animate and inanimate resources that operate online and in real time to help in the endeavour. Expansion and success are in your mindset. The right mental attitude generates favourable results.

And, even in the face of adversity, the positive approach enables you to make the most of manifested choices. This works as an antidote for stress and related health problems.

Positive thinking is contagious. It has the power of latching on to everyone we meet and interact with. A healthy mindset reflects in body language, aura and mood. The application of positive thinking may not always be possible without some external guidance and stimulation. It is for this very reason that a number of books and workshops on motivation have been designed. With the initial thrust, it is easy to visualize and work towards favourable situations.

The Different Faces of Positivity

Positivity is not a Pollyanna-ish rose-tinted view of things which ignores reality, but a choice we make about thinking, acting, and speaking which creates reality. As such, it has the power of magic.

Positive thinking can change your life if you are prepared to train yourself into making it a habit. If you want to succeed more often in any of your ventures in life and work, you need to get the Positivity Habit. Some of the ways to achieve success through positive thinking are as follows:

Create a Positive Self-Image through your Self-Talk

Your self-image is the person you think you are and which is your own creation. When your self-image is low, you attract into your life all the experiences and conditions that tell you how poor you are. Conversely, when your self-image is high, you attract experiences telling you how great you are.

The easiest way to create the self-image you want is through your self-talk. Simply control the chatter in your head. Boost your morale regularly, morning, noon, and night with what you tell yourself.

Talk in Terms of Positive Goals

Our brains need images of positive goals to work towards. They become confused if we feed them negative goals. So, if it is your aim to give up smoking, don't say, "I want to stop smoking." Instead, say, "I want to enjoy a pleasant evening out with a couple of refreshing drinks, breathing in fresh, revitalising, clean, pure, uncontaminated, healthy air."

Have Positive Expectations

Numerous experiments confirm the truth that when you expect the best, you usually get the best, and when you expect the worst, you usually get that too. This is known as the self-prophesying principle.

So, at the start of any new enterprise or at the start of each new day, look forward with expectations of the very best.

Always Review Positively

If we are positive at the start of an enterprise, we should be equally positive at the end when we review. Many people become discouraged when things don't go according to plan and they beat themselves up for missing out on the one thing that didn't work. But there are always gems of real worth in every situation, even apparent disasters, if we only look hard enough.

One way to review positively is to use igniter phrases rather than chloroform phrases. So, an obstacle is not a "barrier" but a "challenge"; a setback is not a "disaster" but a "chance to learn"; and a tough problem is not a "failure", but "a nut we're going to crack".

Mix with Positive People

One of the biggest drains on our enthusiasms is to be surrounded by people who are negative. They may be well-meaning with their warnings but they are misguided. You have two choices if you want to survive as a positive person: avoid them or train them.

One clever way to train negative people is to simply ignore

them when they use discouraging conversation. Simply blank them. Then when they return to positive expressions, re-connect. Very soon, they will learn that you are a person who has a sunny disposition and they will simply drop their previously gloomy attitude with you.

Use Positivity for Good Health

A number of studies proved that positive thinking can cure both mental and physical pain. Scientists have found that a positive attitude was one of the key ingredients of long living.

More recent studies have shown that brain cells actually shrivel up and die under the effect of negative thinking, while positive thinking actually changes the composition of body cells for the better. This all goes to show that positivity is better than any medicine you could buy from the chemist store.

Get the Positivity Habit

Good habits are as easy to make as bad ones. It's simply a matter of choice and repetition. So, if you want the positivity habit in your life, do these things everyday:

- dress the best you can
- smile more
- try to genuinely like others
- give people positive strokes of recognition

- give people the most precious gift you have: more of your time
- be thankful for everything you get.

Handling Children Positively

Tips for Handling Children

Raising kids is a difficult, yet important task. You can end with a happy and valuable member of our world or an unhappy problem for society to handle.

Even if you are not currently raising children, they are a big part of your future. Remember that today's children are tomorrow's leaders.

The effect you have on children is enormous. You may not think your actions are shaping their lives, but the end result tells the story.

Here are a few quotes to help you by a renowned author:

While raising kids, think about, "Who were the adults in your own childhood? Who were your favourite relatives? Your favourite leaders, sports coaches or teachers?" If you smile at the memory, they probably treated you like a friend, not a child.

Try to find out what a child's problem really is and without crushing their own solutions, try to help solve them.

A child is a regular person in a small body. You don't own a child. He or she is starting to think. If you encourage them to solve problems, you are building their confidence. For example, asking the right questions is often more valuable to people than giving out answers.

Ask them, "Why are you crying? Why was he mean to

you? What do you want to do about it? Okay. What might be a better way to solve it?"

Observe them-and this applies even to babies. Listen to what children tell you about their lives.

For example, you might observe that a baby calms down when a football game is on the television. You discover your three-year-old gets excited when painting pictures.

An eight-year-old may tell you something you've never considered. As well as making children feel heard or observed, you learn things as well.

Let them help-if you don't, they become overwhelmed with a sense of obligation which they then must repress.

How do you feel if someone gives you money or favours, but refuses to let you return the favour in any way. You might think you have nothing of value for that person. If you are not allowed to help the person back, you'll soon dislike or distrust the person and refuse all future gifts.

Try saying, "If you fold the napkins, it would really help me"; "I'll give you an allowance if you take care of all the garbage for the house"; "You'd help me feel happier if you sang a song for me."

Take care that a child factually does not do well without love. Most children have an abundance of it to return.

Build Healthy Food Habits for a Happy Home

Handling School-going Children

Grade-schoolers can fall anywhere in a wide spectrum when it comes to food preferences. Some may still be picky eaters while others may have become adventuresome gourmands. But no matter what kind of food lover or hater your child is, you can help shape his preferences and attitudes toward food by guiding him toward good food habits.

Go Groceries Shopping Together

Fill your cart with fresh produce and cut down on processed foods. Make a game out of picking different colours of fruits and vegetables.

Think about dishes you can make in the coming week, such as a stir fry (green broccoli, yellow and red peppers, orange carrots, and so on).

Let your Child Help you Cook

Your child may not be able to chop vegetables, but they can certainly tear up lettuce for a salad or put bread in a basket. Your 9 or 10-year-old can stir sauces or measure out ingredients.

You'll be glad you encouraged culinary habits early when your grade-schooler grows into a teen, who can skilfully whip up a delicious dinner for the whole family.

Don't Stress About how much your Child Eats

They may polish off everything on his plate one day and then eat two peas and declare that they are done the next. This is perfectly normal behaviour for a growing grade-schooler.

Make sure you don't make them feel bad for not finishing everything on the plate. Head off problems at the pass by offering smaller portions (you can always give them seconds if they finish).

Encourage Smart Snacking

Even if your child is served a favourite dish for dinner, they may not eat it if they are snacked too close to mealtime and are hungry. Don't let them snack at least an hour before dinner, and if they do, have something, make it as healthy and light as possible.

Avoid the Allure of Bribes

It can certainly be tempting to say no TV, dessert, or whatever else they want unless they eat dinner. But this can create an uneasy relationship with food in your child. Instead of making them feel pressured into eating when they don't feel like it, give them choices that are more likely to go down easy.

Don't Ban Junk Food

This doesn't mean allowing your grade-schooler to eat a candy bar a day. Limiting processed food that's high in sugar and calories is a good idea. But if you try to forbid so much as a lollipop in your home, your child is more likely to scarf up all the sugar they can find at a friend's house.

A better way to handle sugary snacks is to let them have a piece of candy or chocolate once in a while, and if they clamour for something sweet, try to steer them toward healthy snacks, such as nuts with raisins the rest of the time.

Set a Good Example

If you ban your child from drinking soda and then guzzle down a Diet Coke over dinner, it sends a mixed message. Examine your own attitude toward food- do you try healthy recipes or eat fatty foods and then express remorse and worry about your own weight?

If you are willing to find new ways to get creative with healthy choices, your grade-schooler will be more likely to follow in your footsteps.

Patience in Homemaking

There is one quality above all others that influence how relaxed your family will be-patience.

Life without Patience

When we lose our patience, we become frustrated. Our frustration turns into anger and resentment. Family members pick up on such emotions rather quickly, even when you think you're hiding them well. Eventually, you may find yourself acting out your anger actively, such as by yelling or snapping at your family, or passively, such as by ignoring or avoiding your loved ones.

Children who grow up in homes where they often feel like the source of frustration may develop low self-esteem. Low self-esteem may grow into depression, anxiety, and anti-social behaviour.

Parents who frequently feel frustrated often feel like failures as parents, especially when their kids begin to act out in response to their frustration. If a lack of patience continues, everyone ends up feeling stressed out most of the time.

Patience, however, creates an environment of compassion and respect. When you're patient with your family members, it's just as though you are saying, "I respect how you feel because I respect you. I want you to be happy and independent because I love you and want the best for you. I want to help you find your own happiness, so I'm going to slow down and take time to calmly assist you.

Sometimes I do this by doing things for you, such as tying your shoes when you can't do it. Sometimes I do this by teaching you to help yourself, such as helping you take deep breaths to calm yourself down or standing back and waiting for you to learn things at your own pace, in your own way, without my intervening. Sometimes I do this by giving you my attention and sharing in your joy."

When you remind yourself that at the end of the day, all of the important things will still be accomplished (showing love to your family being the most important thing of all), then you can stop rushing and complaining and start enjoying the ride during the ups and downs of life.

Losing Patience

Your children will push you to the limits of patience. They don't mean to do it. Some of those patience killers are just a part of normal, healthy development. Kids just don't realize how their behaviours impact others. When you are in a rush, they will dawdle.

When you want to focus on a project, they will interrupt you. When you simply want a moment of quiet, they will shriek, make annoying sounds, and fight, often for no reason, it seems, other than to disrupt the peace.

When you easily see the solution to a problem, they will argue with you, throwing tantrums at times, because they cannot see the solution at all. Sometimes, it is the child who lacks patience, and that alone can cause you to lose yours.

There will be days when you want to demand compliance. "You will listen to me." "Move faster." "Stop fighting, and leave each other alone." It is effective for the short term, but it loses it's effectiveness over time because it conveys a message to your children that says, "I don't respect you."

Finding Patience

When you're ready to accept that you don't always need to be in charge or on schedule that a few extra moments in your day tending to the emotional needs of your family will actually make things run more smoothly in the end, then you're ready to develop your patience.

Make a point to be patient. You may even set a day or time to start, such as right after dinner. Decide to pay more attention to your family members by focusing on them rather than handling their issues while focusing on something else. Decide to handle things calmly. Even do your best to speak with a delightful voice.

If you catch yourself losing patience (or even if somebody else points it out to you), simply stop, close your eyes, take a deep breath or two (count if you have to), and remind yourself that you are going to try to be more patient because it will make things easier in the long run. Then, calmly address the problem.

Don't let yourself feel guilty for not having patience 100% of the time. Nobody is that perfect. Just be proud of yourself for catching your slip-up and reminding yourself to redirect to a more patient practice.

Having Patience with Troubled Child

Having patience with your child is sometimes the most difficult task that you will ever have to deal with. All children will go through a stage in that all they will do is push your buttons. You are not alone.

You love your children so why are they acting so bad? A simple answer is that they are kids. They all do it. You can fix the problem simply by spending more time with them and a little discipline.

Talk More

The first thing you need to do is talk more with your children. At this stage, it is crucial that you teach them what is right and what is wrong. Communication is the key to success. You do not want to give them the impression that if they whine enough or throw a big enough fit that you will give in and they will get their way.

You need to put your foot down. If you are going shopping you need to plan ahead what you are going to buy. Talk with your child before you arrive at the store so they know what to expect. Then there shouldn't be any surprises when you arrive. If there is, tell them you will have to leave the store. Then you go back at another time without them.

Discipline

Another key item at this stage is discipline. Sometimes it doesn't feel right but you need to have a set way to discipline your children. This way they know what to expect if they do something wrong that they are going to get punished.

Maybe it is as simple as a timeout in the corner for five minutes. Or maybe they cannot play their video games over the weekend. Let your children know that if they continue this behaviour, they will be punished.

Quality Time

Sometimes children act out and are naughty because they feel left out. Have you been spending more time with something else? Is there a new sibling around the house? Having you been putting extra hours in at the office? Some of the littlest changes around the household can make a huge impact on your children.

Make sure you set aside some quality time with each of your children on a daily basis that is just for you and him. A little time goes a long way.

Help your Children be Better People

You love your children with all your heart, however, sometimes they pinch that last nerve and start to turn it. How do you keep your patience and help them all in the same time that is the question on every mothers mind.

Every action that we take as parents effects our children in some way, whether it be how they talk, how they act, or even their esteem. You always want your children to have high esteem, to make them a better person.

Here are a few techniques discipline children whenever our little joys are pinching that last nerve:

- Don't lose your temper with your children. They can sense when someone is upset or when they are angry or whichever the feeling may be. Children have something almost like radar that just picks up on those feelings and it makes them worrisome and anxious causing them to act up more, so whatever you do, keep your calm.

- One simple way to calm down the temper is to take a breather. Take a step back and close your eyes, calm yourself down.

  If you have to, make sure the child is OK, and then walk into another room and calm yourself down for a second and then go back to the child. Never say or do anything out of anger, because that is where hurt feelings come from, and whatever the case you never want to hurt your child in any way.

- Another surefire way to calm yourself down is to count backwards from 20. Get your mind focused on counting and not on the upsetting situation at hand. That will help clear your mind, and help to calm you down. Remember the child is the main focus and the most important so remember to keep it calm.

■ ■ ■

CHAPTER 10

Home Decoration

Designing of a house with blank white rooms and windows with pull down shades does not leave any cue on how to decorate it. A homemaker is the person who adds a character, a personality to the house, which further serves as an extension of her own self, her family and her culture.

She adds that personal touch that makes the house her own home, which puts her at ease in an instant and has an intimacy that makes her feel completely relaxed. To make home cozy, warm and comfortable, we should keep the following points in mind:

- Theme of the room or home can be the guiding factor while decorating it. It is a reflection on our personality, likes, tastes and hobbies and the culture of our family. A chosen theme such as Barbie's Home, Nautical Mile, Star Wars, Period Decor, Nature Lovers and Ethnic, can be the unifying factor for all our furniture, furnishings, accessories, colours of walls and ceilings, windows and doors and even the showcase area to display our collections, arts, crafts and other prized possessions.

- Eliminate things that don't fit into the theme decor of the room or modify them to suit the overall theme.

  This can be a good restraint on impulsive shopping, disproportionate planning or unplanned implementation of decoration items.

- Artifacts that suit the main theme can add a special touch to the room decor such as a small wooden ship to go with the nautical theme.

- All collectors love to display their collections of stamps, coins, dolls or other trinkets in a special creative way.

  Linear arrangements can be dull so may be grouping them and presenting them in interesting ways, such as in glass cupboards will draw more attention to them and to our skill of refinement.

- Colours of walls, fabrics, furniture, linen, pillows, shelves and curtains and type of furniture, beds, sofas and seating arrangements and even accessories, lamps and vases that we use must also confirm with our room or home decor theme.

- Upholstery colours and fabric prints should be used judiciously. Maintain the harmony by using the same or similar accent thrice around the room at least.

Cozy Home Decoration

The most significant aspect of a home is how comfortable it is. To create a comfortable and cozy home, all we need to do is give wings to our creativity and imagination, with a dash of common sense. Warm colours, inviting furniture, subtle decoration and textured draperies goes a long way deciphering the cozy formula of the home.

By arranging such important factors in the right style, we can give a complete makeover the house, changing the mood, look, personality, character and overall environment of a room.

Ideas for Cozy Home Decoration

- The first thing that comes to mind, when we think of cozy home decoration is the colour scheme of the rooms. The most ideal option would be to choose a warm yellow, muted red, or terra-cotta paint colour.

  Another option would be to keep the existing paint intact and just accentuate one of the walls of the room.

- Make use of variety of textures. Soft and fluffy pillows, cushions and throw blankets make the room look cozier, as we can snuggle in them and feel at bliss.

  While baskets and hardbound books arranged neatly in book cases, make the room look more sophisticated and ethnic, black chrome armchairs, metallic round chairs, modern irregular-shaped tables and large mirrors make the room look too formal.

- Remember, when it comes to choosing the colour for creating a cozy room dark warm-toned colours suit the best. Both walls and furnishings, in warm tones, make the room pleasant and inviting.

- Sleek furniture, though occupies less space, make the room look quite formal. Instead, go for textured furniture if we want to create a cozy atmosphere. Do not go for traditional heavy wooden ones.

- The use of more patterns makes the room appear smaller and cozier. However, in case you have a small room, use patterns sparingly.

- Throw rugs add instant warmth to the room and are great for those, who have their house on rent.

- Fluorescent and halogen lights look harsh and are too bright for coziness and warmth in the room. Use soft incandescent lights instead. Candles serve best for the purpose.

  Place various shapes, sizes and colours of candles on tables, mantels, or coffee tables. Candles when placed in front of mirrors bounces light, filling the room with a nice warming effect.

- To add drama to the lighting effect, infuse down lighting and up-lighting in the rooms. While in the former case you can go for lamp shades that diffuse the light down wards, the latter is mostly concerned with attracting the attention to the family photos and portraits on the walls, by installing a light above them.

- Re-arranging the furniture to the focal point of the room

would go a long way in emphasising the 'cozy' factor. Move furniture closer to the fireplace area or near a window that gets lots of sunlight - a perfect place to snuggle around!!

Tools for Home Decorating

Home decoration goes a long way in deciphering the personality and taste of the people living in it. It does not matter whether we are living in a big colonial mansion or a small rented apartment, what matters the most is how we have styled our house. It is very essential for a home to radiate positive vibes and energies to the people staying and also to the guests.

Only then, does a house transform from being just a 'house' to a 'home'. Talking about home decoration, the options are endless. You can either go for warm, comfortable, cozy home or an elegant formal one or the traditional conventional styled decor.

Whatever be the style of the house, there is one thing that you cannot do without - a toolbox. Whether it is budget and 'do-it-ourself' decor projects or for the repair and maintenance of the decor, it is imperative to have a tool box, with all the essential equipments.

Make sure it has all the necessary implements that would be needed for completing a home decor project. The different tools help in various works such as cutting, pasting, storing, accentuating and so on. Here is the checklist that you can use to arrange for tools that you will need for decorating our home:

- A step stool is one of the most essential tools, when it comes to home decorating. The uses of step stool are varied - right from painting ceilings or the top portions of walls, to hanging up curtains, clearing cobwebs, which accumulate over a period of time.

- One cannot ignore the need of a toolbox or caddy. It is essential for storing tools and other small tit-bits.

- Adhesives are quintessential products for home decoration. These include glue guns and sticks, spray adhesive can, staple gun with extra staple boxes, rubber bands, plastic twist ties, fusible interfacings and sewing needles and thread (exclusively used in case of fabric wallpapering).

- For those who have a front or back lawn/garden, gardening tools such as lawn mower, lawn aerators, leaf sweepers, pruning shears, compost turning garden tool, etc are much required.

- Accessories to decorate home, such as gold and silver touch-up pens, black and white spray paints, paint brushes and colours, sandpaper cannot be missed, when gathering tools for home decoration. Sometimes buttons, ribbons, laces and fringes are also required.

- If you want to hang pictures, messages and other things on the wall such as cup hooks, thumb tacks, push pins, plastic anchors, picture wire, and plastic anchors

- Sharp tools such as box cutter, cutting pliers, utility scissors and fabric scissors are essential requisites when it comes to home decoration.

- No home decor project can be complete without measuring tools such as yardstick, measuring tape, T-Square or level and so on.

- In case you are getting woodwork done to revamp the look, woodworking tools, such as a lightweight handsaw, screwdrivers of all sizes, C-clamps, nails and hammer, are required.

Solutions for Room Decor Problems

Room decor is not as easy as it seems at the first sight. One may fancy that glamorous room in the home decor magazine but may find it almost impossible to translate into a reality because of the simple reason that the construction of our home and measurement of our rooms is entirely different.

You may be renting an apartment where you cannot redo the positioning of walls, doors and windows or have a large hall. Colour, lines and furniture arrangement can make a huge difference to your room decor. Once you have identified the most common problems that people often face while doing room decor, you can come up with solutions.

Tips for Very Long Room

- The best way to deal with a very long room is to split it into two using screens and room dividers that we may use as study area, living area, dining room, personal gym or just entertainment room.

- Use warm dark colours on shorter walls to make them advance and give the room a balanced look.

- Define separate areas by using different area rugs.

Tips for Low Ceiling

- Long curtains that can be draped from above the door level and window level all the way to the floor, add height to the room.

- Paint ceiling in light cool colour to make it recede and add light to the room.

- Tall accessories, such as lamps, look good and make room look taller too.

- Add height to a room by installing vertical and tall cabinets or bookcases in the room.

Tips for Narrow Room

- Any linear arrangement on shorter walls, such as placement of shelves, art pieces or rugs, will make them look wider.

- Diagonal arrangement of furniture looks better.

- Fool the eye by painting longer walls in cool light colours to make them recede.

Tips for Tall Room

- Horizontally placed shelves, crown mouldings and art pieces cut off the height of the room.

- In such rooms, ceilings should have a warm dark colour.

- Play the visual trick of installing the mouldings or chair rails to one half to three quarters of the way up the walls.

Tips for Very Big Room

- Experiment with warm and dark colours on walls to make the room look cozier and friendlier.

- Group furniture pieces into two or more separate seating arrangements.

- Like long rooms, big rooms can also be divided into smaller areas using screens and room dividers and can be used for better purposes and will make the room look cozier too.

Step by Step Decor

Home Decor can be quite an overwhelming task with all those measurements, planning, wall colours, ceiling colours, type, colour and size of furniture, furnishing colours and patterns, size of rugs, storage areas, cabinets and so many things to keep in mind. It is an expensive task too. To make home decor easier and more manageable, it is advisable to make a time and budget schedule and decorate home step by step.

Narrow down the focus to one corner at a time and complete home decor as a series of projects that are not too taxing on time, energy and budget. This will also be rewarding as completion of one project will relieve of that portion of home decor and motivate with success and the beautiful change.

While doing the entire room at once seems to be a daunting task, making a cozy corner in the living area as the focal point of the room may be achieved by placing a coffee table, chairs around it and arranging flowers in a vase on the table. Here are some tips for step-by-step room decor:

- Choose a really attractive art piece or feature to make it the focus of attention in the room.

- Lend the dramatic touch and personality to room by setting focal point around the piece which has been chosen.

- Every year, invest in one single but visually appealing piece of furniture.

- A fashionable sofa in attractive colours with pillows and a throw in complimentary colours can add new life to living room.

- Improvise a long wall or an unused corner by placing an antique chest or armoire there and beautify them using a collection of displayable china, glass or pottery.

- Drawers and shelves are always needed to store linens and many other household items and can be carved out in any unused area and long-forgotten corners of the home.

- Remove the clutter that gets collected on the table and keep the items needed in drawers. A study lamp or a personal computer, a pen stand, a paperweight and a small notepad should be enough for daily use. Keep it simple and organised.

- Keep the dining room simple too. It should be friendly, warm and its furnishings should be versatile that can be style according to the occasion and changing trends.

- Try flexible dark coloured furnishings that can be brightened up with using sparse modern art accessories.

- Light-finished wood can be infused with new life by adding greenery or ceramics and glass collectibles.

- Be as creative as we like in master bedroom that makes our feel pampered, happy and relaxing. Invest in a really good bed and make it the centre of attention.

- Other features of the bedroom should be rather kept muted and dress the bed with stylish linen in beautiful hues, prints and patterns and spare functional accessories.

- Do-it-ourself features, such as sewing up upholstery for home or giving a new look to an old ottoman or a table and making a stylish lampshade not only makes home look better but also gives artistic satisfaction. Try them out.

The Science of Colours

We all know that all colours are made up of three primary colours - red, blue and green - in various combinations. Secondary colours are made up of mixing of these primary colours, such as cyan; yellow and purple while tertiary colours are made up of mixing the secondary colours to the primary colours, such as reddish orange and yellowish green. Absence of all the three colours make up an absolute black, which is almost non-existent, and the black we normally talk about is actually a tint or shade of the actual colour.

Similarly all these three colours mixed in equal parts would produce pure white light. Colours that we are talking about are actually the light particles reflected by a substance when the source absorbs the rest of it. It is actually the tints, tones, values and shades of the basic key hues that make our world so colourful to look at.

- Hue means Colour such as red colour or red hue.

- Tint means the pure colour mixed with white such as tints of red means red mixed with white colour to produce different kind of reds and pinks.

- Tone of a colour means that the pure colour is mixed with grey.

- Value of a colour means the lightness and darkness of a shade achieved by the sheer or deeper application of the colour.

- Key colours are the dominant colours that we have chosen for room or home decor.

- Shade of a colour means that the pure colour is mixed with black.

While painting walls and ceilings or deciding a colour scheme for home decor, it is always helpful to collect chips and swatches of favourite colours from various sources, such as fabrics, hardware stores and even cuttings that you can arrange and rearrange to decide what colours look good together. Furnishings are a wonderful way to add colour and texture to our home and can be moved easily too.

Choosing Colour Schemes

Colour scheme helps us to determine the harmony between colours in home decor. A colour wheel can be quite useful while deciding a colour scheme for home, as it helps us to compare complimentary colours.

Interactive colour wheel tools and software are available online for our reference. The use of colour wheel makes choosing the combination of colours for painting our walls, accents, furnishings, furniture and accessories much easier. Here are a few tips that we can use while deciding upon the colour scheme for home:

- Monochromatic colour scheme uses only one colour throughout. Variety is introduced by using various tints, tones, values and shades of that key colour and different textures.

- Complimentary colour scheme uses two colours placed opposite to each other on the colour wheel, their tints, tones, shades and values, such as yellow and violet. This scheme is quite bold and lends a dramatic touch to the home decor.

- Analogous colour schemes use three hues placed adjacent

to each other on the colour wheel, but use either combination of warm colours only or combination of cool colours only.

- Triadic colour schemes use three hues placed consecutively or at equal distances from each other such as red, yellow and blue, their tints, tones, shades and values

A novice can easily decide upon the colour scheme using the following steps:

- Use favourite pattern as the guiding line for our colour palette. The lightest colour in the pattern can be used for the background, such as wall paint colour, medium colour for large furniture pieces, windows, doors, closets and cabinets while the darkest colour can be used for accessories.

- Colour can make quite a lot of difference to the size and proportion of the room. So, remember that white and pale colours reflect light more to making the room appear larger, while dark colours make room appear cozier and smaller.

- When it comes to furniture and accessories, white and pale coloured objects or objects in similar colour as the wall recede into background while brighter and darker objects attract attention more and seem to occupy more space, so if the room is really small, try buying furniture and furnishings in same colour as walls or pale shades and accessorise with bright bold colours to create focal points.

Small Space Living

For efficient small space living, keep in mind the area available

at all times. Multi-
functional furniture
pieces and furnish-
ings that optimize
usable space quite
effectively are the
beat for such rooms.

Here are some tips:

- An elevated loft
  bed is a great
  item to make use of vertical room space while open
  shelves instead of chest of drawers can be used to
  accommodate more books and magazines.

- Display handmade quilts and throws that make the bed
  look warm and elegant at the same time.

- Fashionable bright-coloured washable slipcovers can
  make mismatched furniture pieces look coordinated and
  in harmony with each other.

- Keep things you want to hide away from view in
  containers that can be stored under the bed.

- Make tiny bedroom look comfortable and inviting by
  adding soft pillows of all sizes and shapes.

- Maximize the use of vertical wall space by adding
  bookcases and shelves.

- Nail some hanging wall shoe pockets at the inside of
  closet door, where you can keep shoes, socks, gloves and
  even handkerchiefs.

- Use bright colours and make use of fabrics complimenting
  bed linens, throws and pillows, to add a romantic touch
  to your tiny home, apartment or dorm decor.

- Use filing cabinets and decorated stackable crates as a cheap option for keeping your place organised.

- Use large storage trunk as a table.

- Add personal touch to tastefully decorated tiny home by selecting a colour scheme for our walls, furniture and furnishings beforehand.

- Utilize space underneath the loft bed by accommodating entertainment area or work desk underneath it along with a beautiful floor lamp and ottoman to rest tired legs.

  Even this ottoman can have the storage area to hide away magazines and bills to be paid.

- Add a small futon for an additional seating area.

More Ideas for Decorating Small Homes

Living in a small space is tough, especially when you have to abide by the rental rules formulated by our landlord. Moreover, decorating options are very less, since one cannot experiment much with the limited space.

However, you can make a small apartment look as beautiful and spacious as its larger counterparts. All you need is to create the illusion of space by arranging the furniture and knowledge about the appropriate lighting, colour of the walls etc.

Small Apartment Decor Ideas

- Furniture plays a pivotal role in every home decor. The choice of home furnishings can either create or occupy space.

- Do not go for bulky sofa sets, because they are difficult to move, occupy a whole lot of space and make the room look cramped. Small pieces of furniture, such as an ottoman, an armless open chair, low table will open up the space. A frugal option is sofa-cum-bed, which can be unfolded to serve as a bed during the night.

- The arrangement of furniture is another thing to consider. Make sure that you place the largest piece of furniture, probably the couch, against the longest wall of the room.

  Keep the furniture away from the walkways, so that people do not stumble upon it while coming or going out of the room.

- Lighting is another important factor in determining the look of the room. For a small apartment, the rooms should be illuminated in such a way that space is opened up. Ceiling lights are a strict no-no in this case, because they tend to cut off the height of the room.

  Soft lighting is preferable. Go for recessed lighting. Install more lamps. Eliminate shadows at the corners of the rooms by placing soft incandescent lights at strategic locations.

- Apart from artificial lighting, natural light also plays a pivotal role in creating the illusion of space. Open the windows of the room during daytime, so that they are illuminated with sun's rays.

- Soft, monochromatic colour schemes create the illusion of more space.

  Hence, choose colours that are light, such as white, cream and off white. You may also opt for cool colours. Select soft tones of blues and greens for the walls.

- Match the walls with a monochromatic colour scheme

for the fabrics of the furniture and drapery. You may choose light and airy fabrics for the throw pillows and curtains. Cotton is the best bet. Laced curtains are good, because they provide good ventilation as well as allow the light to pass through, during the day.

- Mirrors can open up a considerable amount of space, because they reflect light. Use large decorative mirrors for the purpose.

- Use minimal number of accessories for your rooms, because they create clutter. Stick to small sized throw pillows, wall hangings and framed photographs or artwork.

- Last but not the least - keep your home free of clutter. Organise things on cupboards, closets and drawers.

  When things are neatly arranged and out of sight, the space in the home is opened up automatically.

Maximising Storage Tips

Today, the market is virtually flooded with furniture and storage systems that can help make the most of the space available at home for storage and work. You can also maximize the storage space by finding the hidden storage areas of your home.

Here are some tips and ideas on maximising the storage of home.

Hidden Storage Ideas

- The first step is to get rid of all the clutter. Collect the old and unwanted stuff that have been occupying a whole lot of space in our drawers, cupboards and closets in your home, and dispose them off.

That way, you will ensure that all the storage areas are occupied by only the useful stuff.

- Furniture is some of the most visible, but 'hidden' storage spaces. For instance, a bed frame with a small shelf can be a nice storage options, which could store small pieces of clothing like undergarments, socks and toys of our kids. We may also purchase boxed bed, which can be used to store heavy blankets and other stuff.

- Apart from books, you may store our office files and stationery items in your bookshelf.

- Make use of shelves and vanity cabinet for storing bathroom essentials and grooming products in the bathroom.

- Instead of heavy, bulky chairs, use ottomans with storage area underneath them. Another nice option is a bar stool set, which can be stacked in the corner when not in use.

- Dressing table is a hidden storage space. You can include slide-in drawers or shelves in the dressing table, to give more space for the cosmetics and our accessories. If there is any space left, you can also store old magazines in them.

- To maximize storage in bathroom and kitchen, make the best use of under-sink areas in the rooms.

- Talking about kitchen, the place can look cramped by the wrong use of storage space. Use vertical slide-in shelves in the kitchen to hang pots and pans.

- Large, sealable plastic vacuum bags are the best options for storing clothing and bedding. They are versatile storage systems, because the air inside the bags can be sucked out using a vacuum, in order to make them smaller and easy to fit into places. You may store them under your bed.

- Multi-function furniture can be the best bet to store electronics, without creating clutter. Make use of such a furniture to store television, music system and DVD player.

  You may get a furniture that has storage space for the electronics as well as some areas designated for storing small items like CDs.

Tips for Keeping Home Organised

Using space effectively is an important art, especially when we are living in small apartments. Know the difference between not having enough space to store things and not making the best use of space. Here are some ideas that we can use to keep our home organised and make the best use of available space:

- A sliding drawer or a shelf can be added underneath a cabinet, furniture pieces or a dresser for greater hidden storage area.

- Desk full of papers and files make work seem overwhelming. So, keep it clear with the help of a full-suspension filing cabinet strong enough to hold all our files away from our view.

- For kitchen cabinets, use plastic multiple-level shelves that can be readjusted easily.

- Furniture pieces with hidden space and storage are an asset for those living in small apartments such as coffee tables and ottomans with storage area underneath or under bed boxes, which are great for keeping quilts and linens.

- If some shelves have too much of space, while others are too full, readjust them according to the space required. Move them a little or add another shelf in between to make more use of the space.

- If you do not have enough space to display all your collectibles at once, rotate them. Put some of your things on display, while store others safely, and then bring them out once a month and replace the things you have displayed already. This will make your home seem new every time someone visits.

- It is very important that you get rid of all the things that you don't like or are not of your use anymore.

- Make best use of wall space by adding shelves, pegboards and corner shelves that can be used to hand up your utensils and tools or display your prizes and collectibles.

- Make use of corner shelves for keeping picture frames or small things in the living room or soap, shampoos, toothbrush and other accessories in the bathroom. They acquire less space and look great.

- Storage units are great when it comes to saving space and being organised. Spices on a spice rack, canned goods in racks, earrings and other small items in cheap ice trays, pens and pencils in a pen stand not only avoid clutter, but are also easier to find when you need them.

- To make more space in the closets, add one rod to hang longer clothing on one wall and two or more rods on the other wall to hang shorter clothing.

- Use common sense and keep things where they are needed most. Remember that china utensils and spices belong to kitchen, toilet paper, napkins and towels to bathroom, lines and quilts to bedroom, videos and CDs to entertainment area and scissors and glue stick to your work area.

  Make space for the things needed in the area there itself, so you don't have to ransack or run over the entire house to search for a thing we need frequently.

- Use portable file boxes to hang the file folders, on-the-desk trays and caddies to keep papers and storage accessories to keep diskettes and CDs.

Bedroom Decor

Architectural elements and focal points in salvage style are fast gaining popularity in bedroom decor for adding class, distinction and sophistication to the room without going over budget. Grecian urns filled with yarn balls look fantastic and quite interesting and

need not cost a fortune too. Here are some tips to lend bedroom a touch of uniqueness and originality within budget:

- Add architectural elements to your bedroom to give it a lavish look such as a fireplace mantel.

- Always look out for opportunities to turn trash and junk into treasure. Old glassware can be used as candleholders, antique cups can be used as votives and blankets can be used as vintage pillows.

- An illustrious wall hanging can take place of a headboard for bed.

- Feel free to use items in different ways other than their traditional uses for the customised touch.

- Hanging old baskets in the nooks and corners of our bedroom will add style to our bedroom and makes creative space for keeping magazines and personal care accessories.

- Ornate birdbaths from someone's fountain can easily be turned into a nightstand or a table centrepiece.

- Salvage antique window frames can be turned into artistic mirror frames.

- Search for some of the most advantageous deals in thrift shops, garage sales and yard sales where we can find home accessories, fabrics, sofa sets and even dinner sets and exquisite items in salvage shops that can be terracotta tiles, ornate wrought iron fences, old pillars and claw foot bath tubs that can make our home look like a heritage property.

- Select a theme for bedroom and only accommodate items that go well with the theme.

- Turn vintage clothing or decorative tablecloths into decorative pillow covers.

- Wrought iron posts and fences can be used as curtain rods.

Romantic Bedroom Decor

Romantic Bedroom Decor has a secret that all interior decorators make use of for that professional-looking lovable huggable cozy bedroom. It is meant to stimulate all the senses. Here are some practical tips to turn your bedroom into a room exuding love and passion:

- A small bar drawer with choicest wines, a Champagne bottle and wine glasses complete the mood of a romantic bedroom.

- Bright harsh lights are a strict no-no for a romantic bedroom decor.

- Choose all our furniture, furnishings and accessories to make the room as intimate and comfortable as possible.

- If you have a sweet tooth, you may keep strawberries, chocolate-dip and whipped cream ready for a late night snack on the dresser too.

- Light up fragrant candles for special occasions to lend that surreal look.

- Make use of those canopy beds and hang sheer light-fabric draperies around the bed to make it ready for your loved one.

- Peaceful romantic bedroom needs silence enough to let you hear your partner's breathing and moaning and block out any other distractions. So keep your television in another room or block out the noise of traffic by hanging thick curtains on the windows.

- Soft romantic music is a must for any romantic bedroom setting. Thus, keep the CD system around for easy use.

- Use opulent red or other bold coloured satin or silk sheets that are soft, have a rich smooth texture and fluffy soft plush pillows.

- Use soft and comfortable mattress that will make you and your partner to plop into the bed immediately.

- Use soft filtered light. You may also use coloured incandescent lights with soft red or pink glow to add romance.

- Use fragrant room fresheners, aromatic incense sticks, scented sachets of soft fragrances, such as lavender and rosemary, or add a thin coat of perfumed oil to your light bulb.

- Sprinkle favourite fragrant powder on bedsheets to make the bed smell sweet and musky.

Furniture Arrangement in Bedrooms

Furniture arrangement in bedrooms is perhaps the easiest part of the bedroom decor and should not be difficult even for the budding home decorators. Here are some handy practical tips that you can use to arrange the furniture in bedroom:

- Start with choosing the wall against which we will place your bed.

- Place your focal point on the opposite side of your bed for maximum visibility.

- Bed placed at an angle in the corner looks quite dramatic.

- A nightstand with drawers and shelves and a lamp can be placed at both sides of the bed for visual balance and allow for place to rest your alarm clock, magazines and books and water. It also allows the couple to have their own reading light in the night.

- Instead of footboards to rest the feet at the end of the bed, you can also place a bench or a trunk that provides versatility enough to be used as seating area and a storage space for blankets and a place to throw your robe after the bath.

- If you have a large master suite, you can use the extra space to create a seating area, reading area or relaxing area for ourself by placing upholstered chairs or a chaise lounge with tall potted plants in the corner for the touch of greenery.

- A dresser with a mirror or a full-length mirror with interesting frame looks quite attractive and is very functional too for nighttime skin care.

- An armoire to accommodate your television, audio systems or books can add the look of lavishness too.

- One or two accent pieces that are unique in finish, colour, material or size can take on the focal point of the room.

- Heirloom-quality furniture may tax your pocket but is worth it. Look for the long lasting and better supporting dovetail joints, durable and easy-to-use metal on metal drawer glides, sanded and stained wood finishes that will keep your clothes safe, cedar-lined drawers for fine clothing and solid brass finish that is always in vogue while buying such furniture.

Bed Types

When we enter into someone's bedroom, the first thing that catches attention is, undoubtedly, the bed. In fact, it is the focus of the bedroom.

Moreover, the decor of the bedroom also depends upon the type of the bed, apart from its positioning, colour, design and size. We can create a lot of difference to the decor of our bedroom, by choosing the right size and type of the bed that fits perfectly into place. The different types of bed available in today's market are designed to provide the ultimate level of comfort, every time we trudge into our bed.

Apart from giving the desired level of comfort and coziness, the beds available today, provide a touch of flair to the decor of the bedroom, thereby enhancing the appearance of the room. In the present times, the furniture stores are stacked with several types of beds, thus providing the flexibility to choose as per one's personal preferences and the decor of the bedroom. There is a wide variety of beds to choose from, which cater to the varying needs of people. You can get the traditional range of beds, as well as those that fit into the contemporary home decor.

Selecting Bed Sheets

Sleeping in bed is the most rejuvenating part of a person's life. So, a comfortable bed and bedding that complements the overall bedroom decor is a must. Since bed sheets are the most visible part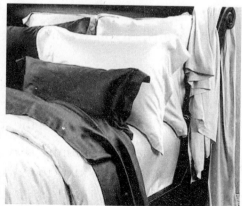

of a bed, high quality bed sheets can make quite a difference to the visual appeal and comfort level of the room.

Here are a few tips on choosing the right kind of bed sheets:

- While most of the mattresses come in standard sizes such as 'King-sized', 'Queen-sized' and 'Full-sized', the customised mattresses with pillow tops and other accessories attached to them can make them larger and wider and will need larger bed sheets than the standard ones available in the market.

  Thus, it is better to measure the bed and the mattress size that you are using beforehand, so that the bed sheets you buy are of appropriate sizes.

- Thread count per inch or TPI is an important factor to be considered while buying a bed sheet. Bed sheets with higher TPI (more than 250) are softer, more comfortable and last longer. The bed sheets having lower than 200 TPI are not recommended for daily use.

- Cotton bed sheets are the most popular ones, though one can use flannel and cotton mixed fabrics as bed sheets depending on taste.

- On the high end of fashion and comfort level, satins and silks with their soft feel on skin win almost every romantic heart.

- Colours and designs of the bed sheets should match the overall theme and colour scheme of the room, though it can have a deeper hue than the colour of the walls.

- Pale colours suit summer season while fall bedroom decor can accommodate more bright and bold colours.

Teens Bedroom Decoration

As the child enters into the teen's age, he doesn't want to be considered a kiddo anymore. At that point of time, children like to maintain the cool image. It is here that the funny colourful toy shaped kids furniture pieces seem to be little absurd to him. The child feels like giving his bedroom a different look that seems to match with his cool funky personality.

Decoration Ideas for Teens Bedroom

Decorating teen bedroom is real fun. You don't need to discard the old furniture. But work upon it to give it a new chic look.

- To begin with, think of a theme for the teen's bedroom.

- The latest fashion is that of retro designs. However, as per your choice, decide whether you would like to go in for modern, retro or cool designs.

- All that is required to be done consists of adding some new accents to the bedroom. Check out some attractive shelves, where you can keep all your stuff. This will help in reducing the clutter, thus giving your room a neat look.

- A very important aspect of bedroom decor consists of a soothing wall colour. Give your walls a new look by painting it with a colour that relaxes our eyes.

- There also arises a need to change the bedroom curtains. Replace the kids ruffled bedroom curtains with the tab-topped curtains in the denim material. That will give the room a more adult look.

- Instead of the vibrant colour cartoon character bed

sheets, shop for some beautiful motif sheets in some neutral colour. As far as the fabric is concerned, check out fabrics like silk or a velvet duvet that is soft to touch and good to feel.

- In case you want to focus the attention on the bed, then for highlighting, check out some prominent prints in bed sheets like that of animals.

- As far the furnishings are concerned, look for things like chairs shaped like a giant shoe or beanbag chairs, fine artwork, funky pillows, exquisite wooden lamps etc.

Kitchen Decor Ideas

Kitchen is one of the most important rooms in the home. Top-class modular kitchens, architectural elements that add lavishness to the kitchens such as crown moldings, latest appliances and stylish hardware and fixtures have become the highlights of today's kitchen.

Kitchen decor has many aspects, such as kitchen shapes and lawet, storage space and colour schemes that have to be paid attention to. Here are some practical tips for kitchen decor:

- Classical kitchen decor uses oak wood.

- Fine-grained woods such as cherry and maple are used for contemporary kitchen decor.

- Mix and match wood finishes and different textures in countertops look interesting and add depth to the room.

- Kitchens can be made traditionally as utilitarian workspaces or as open spaces that are a part of dining rooms or living room.

- While most preferred shape for a kitchen is U-shape to allow the person to make best use of the 'work-triangle' of the space; other popular shapes are L-shaped kitchens, galley-shaped kitchens and island kitchens.

- Stainless steel appliances with pewter finish are most commonly used in kitchens, while silver or gold dinnerware is undoubtedly for grand and lavish dining.

- Glass cabinets to show off your best china and wooden panels to hide the rest are quite popular.

- Space should be reserved to accommodate cooking range, ovens, dishwashers and sinks.

- Make sure that kitchen counters are durable, look beautiful and are easy to clean. Most common are granite, slate and marble slabs and tile mosaics are fast catching up to lend a unique look to the kitchen.

- Kitchen needs the most storage space with lots of hidden storage areas too and we can mix and match rollout shelves, vertical tray dividers and pullouts and drawer inserts. You will also need recycling bins and appliance garages.

Kitchen Floors

- It's important to choose flooring material consistent with the rest of the home. Tile is distinctive, but it can be cold if not heated underneath and its hard surface may require an area rug in work areas where prolonged standing occurs.

- Kitchen flooring in bold colours are vibrant and energetic but expensive too. Neutral colours are the traditional choices and more budget-friendly too.

- Recessed adjustable lighting and decorative lighting fixtures spotlighting our kitchen island or dining area can add a dramatic effect to our kitchen decor.

Kitchen Cabinet

The first thing that grabs our attention in others' kitchen is undoubtedly the kitchen cabinet. It is the most prominent piece of furnishing in the kitchen. On one hand where it acts as a great storage, on the other hand, it acts as means to adorn our kitchen and give it a livelier look.

- Coming up in different shapes and sizes, these kitchen cabinets are selling like hot cakes. There are plenty of places where you can look out for different kinds of kitchen cabinets like the cabinet showrooms, lumberyards and home improvement centers.

- Talking about the kitchen cabinet style, there is a large diversity available, ranging from the basic wooden cabinets to the advanced modular ones. You can either purchase them from the furniture stores or else get it customised by hiring the services of a professional cabinetmaker.

- Measure the lawet of your kitchen and accordingly decide what size would the best for our cabinet. The markets are stocked with cabinets of different sizes.

  In terms of width, you can find the cabinetry ranging from 9 inches to 48 inches, at an increment of 3 inches. In terms of finish and style, the cabinet stores offer a vast range.

- Keeping in mind the theme of your kitchen, you can choose to go in for contemporary laminated ones or the traditional hardwood style. Even in wood, you can find various kinds of material, differing in quality. There are mainly two types of kitchen cabinets, namely, the face frame and the frameless.

Kitchen Furniture and Accessories

One of the best ways to add style and grace to a kitchen is through furnishing and accessorising it. Remember, right accessories and furniture can entirely transform your kitchen into the most pleasurable area of our home.

Right from major decisions, such as placement of refrigerator, kinds of counters and cabinets installed, to the smallest detailing, such as the kind of knobs, handles and hinges used, there are a lot of things you need to consider, when it comes to styling your kitchen. The quantity, size and theme of the kitchen accessories must match with the decor theme and space available. Here are some ideas for furnishing and accessorising the kitchen:

- Once decided on the colour of walls, placing of refrigerator, counters and cabinets, categorise all accessories by colour, size or style and then choose them according the scale and visual balance.

- Install the largest accessories first, keeping the aesthetic balance, right eye level, distance to the cooking area, and then move on to the smaller ones.

- Wall clock is a must in the kitchen, whether you are a student, working person or a housewife, so that you can get done with cooking on time. It also helps to monitor your cooking better.

- Designer range hoods do not only look trendy, but are also quite functional, when it comes to get rid of smoke and vapours.

- Kitchen carts & worktables come in quite handy for a variety of things and can be moved or folded and slipped under the counter after use.

- Pot racks and baker's racks are for those with advanced culinary skills.

- Covered trashcans are a must in the kitchen to discard all those soda bottles and boxes.

- Cabinet accessories, designer sinks, faucets, knobs and pulls lend a sophisticated look to the kitchen.

- Stools and chairs that can be stacked on top of the other can be used and then stacked in the corner in a small kitchen.

- Chopping blocks and countertops are a must, but you may also opt for wine racks.

- Decorate your appliances too with beautiful decorative panels.

- Stainless steel wall shelves and backsplash accessories are the latest trend in kitchen decor.

Kitchen Colours

Colours bring life to any object. Thus apart from making the kitchen an exciting place to be in, they also revamp the look completely, also at a minimal cost. Creative use of colours can result in a budget-friendly kitchen decor that can stimulate your hunger and punk-up your surroundings.

Right from the mottled, textured neutrals - whites, grays and black to the silver metallic, the options are varied and endless. Materials like corian, granite, laminates, stainless steel and tiles are another way to spice up your kitchen.

Kitchen Colour Ideas

- One of the most efficient ways to add colour to a kitchen would be to paint the kitchen cabinet. Since cabinets usually occupy the greater part of the kitchen, adding colour to them would be a great way spice up the kitchen decor.

- For the kitchen walls, the best bet would be to install new tiles in trendy designs and deep tones all over the kitchen or above the kitchen counters. Apart from looking beautiful and colourful, tiles make cleaning and wiping easy and simple.

- A monochromatic colour scheme with matching cabinet, countertop and wall colours can be spiced up by creating a focal point in the kitchen in bold contrasting colours and stenciled motifs.

- Another area of concern for beautifying a kitchen would be to install bright, multihued curtains available in decorative patterns. However, get curtains that are easily washable.

- Do not overlook the fact that colours look different in different lighting systems. If you are planning to go for fluorescent or incandescent lighting, it may affect the hue of our kitchen colour in a different fashion entirely.

- Since lighting affects the colour greatly, the best bet would be to go for recessed and cabinet lighting plan in the kitchen rather than the uniform lighting plan. The former would give a diffused light to the kitchen and also make it look brighter and appealing.

- Add a dramatic touch to kitchen decor by using light and shadows to compliment the kitchen colours. A spotlight above our cooking area and dining area may actually make your simple kitchen look like a studio kitchen.

- Besides the cabinetry, ceiling, floor and window coverings, moldings and trim, there are other design elements too such as chandeliers and designer lights, knobs and pulls, hanging plates and pot racks.

- Using colour in accessories, flowers, jars, vases, pendant light shades, bar stools, pictures and so on are great ways to provide focal points and pockets of colour.

Designer Kitchen

The term designer kitchen is often perceived differently by different people. There are many people who perceive it to be the privilege of the elite class, who can hire the services of experts from the interior decorating world and include all the latest appliances in their kitchen.

Then, there is the second category of people, those who consider a designer kitchen to be nothing more than a replica of the kitchens that adorn the houses of celebrities. Yet another category of people consider designer kitchen to be a kitchen that we design for our own sweet home, right from the scratch level.

In actuality, designer kitchen is a kitchen that follows all the trends that are prevailing in the present times, at the same reflecting our personality. Planning a designer kitchen, though not a daunting task, surely requires everything to be planned very carefully.

You need to lay emphasis on each and every small detail of the kitchen and give it a personal touch as far as possible. While laying down your designer kitchen, keep one thing in mind - you need to achieve near perfection in almost every aspect of the decor.

There are a number of styles in which you can organise a designer kitchen. While selecting one for your kitchen, make sure that it imparts a welcoming, warm and cozy look to the room. Employ only those equipments and installations that we either have use of or are quite sure of using in the near future.

A crowded kitchen will never look inviting and will create unnecessary bothers for we, while working. Remember, your kitchen should give a feeling of comfort and reflect your style statement as well as your personal taste.

Things in a Designer Kitchen

Apart from the basic items, like latest cooking range, chimneys, built-in drawers and cabinets, there are certain other aspects that you need to consider, while going in for a designer kitchen.

- If you have the space and the budget for it, having a pot filler faucet in your designer kitchen is a good idea. Since the faucet is mounted on the wall, along side your stove or above the sink, it is also known as wall mount faucet.

- While selecting the sink for your designer kitchen, there are two options that gain immediate attention - Copper Farmhouse Sinks and Glass Kitchen Sinks.

  Depending upon the overall decor of the house, you can choose between the two options, both of which are practical to use and impart the perfect 'designer' look to your kitchen.

- In the present times, normal convection ovens are just so passe. Ruling the roost today are 'trivections', which make use of conventional, convection and microwave technologies for cooking purposes, in turn reducing the time required for preparing an entire meal.

- The latest entrant in the range of designer kitchen appliances comprise of the 'induction cooktops'.

  As you move over to the newest sensation, leaving behind the standard cooktops and ranges, our cooking time will come down drastically.

- If you shy away from grilling just because the barbecue is placed, it is time to make way for an indoor grill. It provides with the option of grilling anything, anytime, within the closed confines of our kitchen.

  Two of the options in this context are open grills, which operate like an outdoor grill, and contact grills, on which you can grill on both sides - at the same time.

- In case you are planning to go for a designer kitchen, but do not have too much space, then going for a built-in microwave drawer is a very good option.

You will be able to reap all the benefits of a microwave, without consuming any space.

Country Kitchen

Based on the concept of simplicity, this type of kitchen decor is great to look at and easy to maintain. In fact, in the contemporary times, more and more people are resorting to country style kitchen design,  mainly because of the welcoming appeal that it holds. Right from the early morning tea to the late night coffee, you would want to have almost everything inside the kitchen itself, reveling in its warmth and comfort.

Colours

One of the first things that you need to keep in mind, while designing a country style kitchen, comprises of colours for the walls as well as the ceiling. Apart from the usual earth tones, like browns and tans, you can go for the subtle shades of green, red, pink, purple and blue.

You can also use grey, black and white, though in moderation. Patterned wallpaper, with a country print, and solid colours, with country themed wallpaper border, are some other options.

Flooring

As far as the flooring of a country style kitchen is concerned, the best options would comprise of natural wood, flagstone and tiles. You can also go in for laminate flooring. In case you have some other type of flooring and cannot afford to change it, then adding country style area rugs or old fashioned braided rugs is a good option. If possible, get themed country rugs, adorned by sunflowers or roosters.

Storage Space

In a country kitchen decor, no additional storage space is provided; rather it is built-in, as a part of the overall decor. Get wooden cabinets with a glass door, so that you are able to show off the country decor items.

An old fashioned, wooden corner cabinet, hutch, or baker's cabinet are some other spaces that you can use for storage purposes. For keeping small items, keep rustic looking baskets at strategic points, throughout the kitchen.

Furniture

Incorporating wicker furniture, as in the furniture made from natural wood or fibre, in your country style kitchen is a good idea. You can also go for an old fashioned bench or rocking chair. For antique looking furniture, with the worn out look, try to visit the local yard sales. If you don't want to replace your existing furniture, then check out some new slip covers, in floral or other country motifs.

Displaying Collectibles

One of the best things about a country style kitchen is that you need not buy new items to decorate them. Old quilts, colourful pottery, and old crocks and bowls will serve as the perfect adornments for such a kitchen.

In fact, all the country memorabilia that you've collected

over the years will go a long way in imparting the perfect country look to our kitchen.

Accessories

Be it the country decor or the modern decor, accessories go a long way in adding to the charm of a room, including the kitchen. In your country style kitchen, use lots of accessories, each of which reflects your personal taste and identity.

For instance, you can hang family pictures, in wooden photo frame, over the walls, or cover the windows with silky lace curtains.

Living Room Decor

In the past, living room or the parlour was the place with formal settings to welcome the honoured guests. With times, it has evolved into a multifunctional room meant to welcome guests, sit and relax comfortably while reading a good book or watching TV, spend some time with the family, chat and gossip with friends and for entertainment.

The most common furniture pieces found in the living room are sofas, love seat, sofa with chairs in different combinations, coffee table, end tables, ottomans, benches, shelves and perhaps a desk and bookshelves. If the living space is also used as a family room, you can also find TV and entertainment centre in the room along with accessories, lighting, art and crafts on display and may be carpets.

An extra large living room may accommodate a piano, eating area complete with dining table, tennis or billiard table or even a number of plants, if the living space receives lots of direct sunlight. We may also shift an armoire to make use of the extra space for storage purposes. Living room can use maximum number of furnishings and it is a challenge to fit in all the desirable furnishings and accessories and coordinate them with carpeting, wall colour, crown moldings, lighting style and window treatments among many other things.

Usually, sofa or the entertainment centre is the largest piece of furniture in a living room and since, placement of sofa will decide the view and focal point for the people seated in the living room, use it as the starting point for living room decor.

Express your personality, your personal taste and decorating flair in the way you decorate your living room. Remodelling or decorating your living room doesn't just mean to throw away items and add furniture pieces to the living room, but how you arrange what you already have in the room. Arrangement mistakes can ruin the look of your room.

Do not go wild with imagination. Some of the rules and traditional ways of keeping things and proper design must be followed to keep things sane. Creative and unusual living room decorating ideas should be limited by the comfort and usability of the room to make the living room more inviting.

Designing in innovative ways that 'break the rules' can be tricky, so it is best left to professionals. Ensure that you maintain visual balance and harmony while displaying your accessories and should not look chaotic. For budget decorating, try to use what you already and then only opt to buy new things that you think are absolutely necessary. See, if rearranging furniture and accessories can achieve the effect we want. For a dream living room, it is not necessary to start from scratch. Make sure that you do not let your precious collection of art lie waste or ignored just because you didn't think of placing them correctly.

Home Decoration

While decorating a living room, one must pay attention to the natural focal point of the room, lifestyle of the family members, functional placement of furniture, creating well-defined traffic patterns, creating close grouping and intimate conversational areas, visual balance, ambient lighting, colour scheme of the room and fabric patterns of the curtains, window treatments and the upholstery.

You must also watch out for organising things, display of accessories, camouflaging architectural elements that are ugly, hanging art and wall groupings, proportion and scale of decoration, unifying factor of your decoration and most importantly, when to stop.

Living Room Furniture

Living room furniture represents personality of the owner of the house. Living room furniture set normally consists of sofas, coffee table, futon chairs, home theatre system and perhaps display cabinets and dressers. Other living room furniture pieces include side tables, futon beds, bean bags and bean chairs among many other things.

The big furniture of the living room and living room furniture sets are not always affordable and setting up a budget is very important, if your pocket is something you need to think about. Know the exact measurement of the living room, and then decide on the size of sofa and other pieces of living room furniture that you should buy.

While large living rooms may be able to accommodate a corner sofa too, smaller living rooms do well with one sofa with tall plants, floor lamps and decorative stands on either side. Buy furniture pieces that match with each other and stick to the colour scheme of the living room. Match the colour of living room walls with the colour of living room furniture to create a uniform harmonious look. When you buy expensive pieces of furniture such as leather sofas and teakwood tables, be sure to check for warranty period offers. A clearance sale may offer some of the best deals. Lighting can give a new look to the living room furniture, so pay attention to it.

Infuse new life to a corner of the living room by placing decorative plants in beautiful stands. People on a tight budget looking for cheap and affordable living room furniture may want to explore the option of buying secondhand furniture.

People often sell their furniture while redecorating their living rooms and the first place to try is to go to look for cheap living room furniture is a secondhand shop. These shops can offer some very good deals for first time buyers, college students and people who are renting. Consignment shops that buy single pieces of used furniture from private owners may also offer the unique pieces that we may love.

The furniture here is cheap. Since the furniture is not being produced and bought from the previous users of the furniture, chances are that there are no or few chances of duplicate furniture designs that can be bought from here. You may ask the manager of these shops to keep you updated or inform you when he gets a furniture piece that matches your requirement.

Sometimes secondhand furniture may not look appealing, but a little restoration and refurbishing can make it look attractive and as good as new. You can paint the old furniture or add new upholstery to it to change the look of your living room furniture and match it with your living room walls or colour scheme.

Leather living room furniture set is quite popular for

greater comfort, elegance and classic style. It suits well to a manly living room decor theme and is most preferred by bachelors. Leather living room furniture can include leather sofa, leather loveseat, leather chairs and even leather coffee table and leather side tables.

They are quite long lasting and look quite stylish, lending a formal look to your living room. Besides the usual living room furniture paraphernalia, the other furniture pieces you may like in your living room are ottomans, entertainment units, armoires, recliners, sectional sofas, sleepers, rockers and gliders. The best strategy to choose living room furniture is to make a furniture lawet before going to the market, so that you know what exactly you want.

Living Room Accessories and Design

Accessorising and designing a living room is to set up a showcase and yet most relaxed space of our house. It sets up the mood of your home and may range from a casual friendly place for our friends to gossip to a most sophisticated and luxurious setting to make a statement to your style and lavishness.

Here are some living room design and modern decor ideas that you can use:

- Throw pillows are important accents for living room decor and can add splashes of bold colours to an otherwise muted colour scheme. They also add warmth and comfort to the living room.

- Area rugs can be used to cover up unattractive areas of carpet and floors and define seating areas of the room. For a large living room, they are a great asset for defining more than one seating areas of the room.

- Painting living room walls with a neutral colour such as white or beige, will leaves you more choices for creating the character of the room while buying furniture and furnishings for the room.

- Layered lighting plan is best for living rooms so that you can spotlight the reading area or the entertainment area, uniform lighting for a casual family gathering and disco lights or accent lighting for party time.

- Media space is fast gaining attention in the modern living room decor and design ideas. Specialty rooms or areas can be created using painted decorative screens in a large room.

- Media spaces are generally painted in deeper shades for intimacy while versatile and multi-purpose areas are generally painted in pale and muted colours.

- Modern living room decor incorporated features such as bookcases with wide shelves for DVDs and collectibles.

- Furnishings, curtains, valances, blinds, cushions and padded seating can add colour, style and pattern to the decor of the room.

Arranging Living Room Furniture

Arranging living room furniture in a right way decides whether your living room looks cluttered and overstuffed or an organised comfortable room where you would like to spend most of your time.

You will learn how to make a living room furniture cozy and see how living room furniture placement can help in making life easier. The first step to plan how to put the furniture in the living room is to measure up the room and draw a sketch of the room on a graph paper using a scale such as ¼ in to 1 ft.

Be sure to mark the location of the electrical points and outlets, telephone point, cable and light switches in the living room to help we know what goes where. You can also use small-scale furniture paper cutouts to see how your living room will look after arranging the furniture.

Choose a focal point of the living room and arrange our furniture and lighting around it. Some of the popular focal point ideas in a living room are a fireplace, a view from the window, window opening out in a garden, a large bookcase, sofa with a special painting hung above it, a home theatre system or big size plasma television.

You may also turn one of the corners of the living room in a focal point using an interesting lamp, tabletop waterfall or other unique decorative pieces on it along with the lighting to highlight it. Set up conversation areas for our guests.

There should be 4 to 10 ft of distance between your sofa or loveseat and chairs, so that people can talk to each other easily. Less than 4 feet of distance will make your living room too cramped, while more than 10 feet of distance between sofa and the chairs will make conversation difficult. Legroom between the sofa, loveseat or chairs and the coffee table should be at least 14 to 18 inches.

Try to make pathway to walk freely in the living room without stumbling on the furniture that is at least 2 to 3 feet wide. Furniture placement and lawet in a small living room can be quite challenging. In a typical apartment living room with space restraints, you will usually find that the entertainment centre is the biggest piece of furniture and has to be placed at the right position first.

Rest of the furniture is set around it. The sofa goes directly opposite to the TV and we may place the chair at an angle. It can be turned around to watch TV or talk to the person sitting on the sofa at our convenience. Two chairs on either side of the sofa will give a balanced look to the room.

In a small living room, the height and mass of the furniture should be too contrasting. A low table against a high back chair can be visually balanced by adding a tall piece of art above it. Do not use bulky cabinets and sleek metallic chairs together. Maintain visual harmony and thematic balance in our living room decor.

Keep the number of the pieces of furniture down to avoid cramped look in a small living room. Use two love seats facing each other instead of four chairs or one sofa and two chairs instead of one loveseat and three or more chairs. Tall living rooms can be subtly divided into separate conversation and work areas by using a sofa or other big piece of furniture that does not need support of a wall to divide up the room.

Living Room Colours

Choosing Living Room paint colours is one of the important starting points of the living room painting idea along with the right type of paint for your living room walls, ceilings and window and door trims. You can get the clues for the colour scheme of your living room from its furniture, window treatments and accessories.

The colours look different in different lights, in daytime and at night, so you may use colour chips and observe them in all possible scenarios to be sure that you get the desired results. If you are still not sure about the paint colour choice for your living room, test it on a small part of the wall and see how it looks like.

This will also tell exactly what the paint will look like because the colour swatches and the actual shade that turns up after painting the walls may slightly differ. You can lend an open and airy look to your living room by installing a chair rail in the room and then paint the lower portion of the wall in a darker colour than the wall above the chair rail.

If you want to hide unattractive trim work in your living room or want a uniform monochromatic look to make it feel more spacious, paint the trimmings, moulds and the walls of the living room in the same colour.

However, if you want to add bold colours as accents to your room or highlight some attractive trim work in your living room, you can use a paint shade lighter or darker than those of the walls to catch the viewer's attention.

While choosing the paint colour for our living room, keep in mind that colours do not always look same on the walls as they do in colour charts of the paint companies. Bright and solid colours can appear lighter or darker than what you had intended depending on their surrounding colours and the amount of light in the area.

Usually, colours appear darker than they really are over a larger surface area, so it is advisable to choose a shade or two lighter than the paint colour you want in your living room.

Strong and warm colours, such as reds, oranges and yellows seem to advance and close a space, making the living room look cozier and more welcoming. Blues, greens and violets are known as cool colours and seem to recede and make a room look larger.

Normally, people paint their living room ceilings in white or off-white to make them look higher and give an airy feeling to the living room.

Medium to dark colours lower the ceiling visually and are good to be used in living rooms that have very high ceilings to make them look cozier. While in small and lower living rooms with ceilings painted in medium and dark colours will look like a dark cave.

Choose a happy colour that makes you feel comfortable throughout the day in your living room. The popular living room colour scheme often uses soft and pastel paint colours in eggshell finish. The living rooms with ample natural light may use darker colours but they should be perfectly balanced with lighter colours so that the room doesn't look too dreary and dark.

Bathroom Decor

Bathroom is not considered just a utility these days. They are seen as the room or space that sets the mood of the rest of your day in the morning, where you can spend some time with just yourself, pamper yourself, and free yourself from the worries of the world. The master bathroom or luxury bathrooms today include at least a toilet, bidet, two sinks, separate tub and shower, whirlpool or spa and perhaps more.

There are half bathrooms that only have a sink and toilet while full bathrooms have bathtub and shower combo along with it. Smaller bathrooms may just have shower area or corner shower stall instead of both tub and shower. Children's bathroom may omit a thing or two but is more colourful and has energetic feel.

Master baths are expanding into personal retreats and spas at home are becoming more and more popular. Whirlpools, Jacuzzi, decorative fixtures and real furniture pieces are becoming a part of luxuries that are incorporated in bathroom design these days. Stainless steel sink, medicine chest, bathtub, shower walls, faucets and spigots are popular in contemporary bathroom decor, though they are available in wide variety of shapes and materials.

Fixtures in white, biscuit or bone colours are popular while chrome faucets with soft brass accents are the latest trend. Artistic and aesthetic sinks, vanity areas, vessel sinks and sinks made up of hand-blown glass are the fashion of the times. Corner shelves, corner shower with shower caddy, hanging towel bars and medicine cabinets with mirrors are all part of the contemporary bathroom fittings including washbasins in regular round, square or rectangular shapes or unique, creative and artistic shapes.

They can be made from stainless steel, glass or ceramic. Steel baths look traditional and are strong and durable while acrylic baths are much more versatile and lightweight. Modern acrylic baths do not feel cold and metallic and are easy-to-maintain.

Bathroom light fixtures range from simple to funky and are available in all colours, shapes and styles and we may add dim soft lights for mood lighting purposes in addition to bright light that we use while applying makeup. Bathroom faucets and other accessories help define the overall style of the bathroom.

Traditional fixtures are more ornate and suit classic, antique, period, shabby chic, colonial, rustic and country bathroom decors while modern fixtures are slim, sleek, angular and ultra-streamlined and look better with high-tech, elite, modern, contemporary and minimalist bathroom styles.

Most of the traditional bathroom accessories have fluting or floral designs while modern pieces have geometric or swirl designs.

Sunken marble, Roman style, claw-foot tubs or bathtubs with elongated pedestal base look classic and formal while a rectangular tub with square tiles or curvy whirlpools suit contemporary bathroom decorations.

Modern and high-tech bathrooms have streamlined pedestal sinks with plumbing on display, vessel sinks or sinks above countertops while traditional bathrooms have marble sinks, vanity-sink combinations or sinks with embellished pedestals. Plain glass, frosted or beaded shower doors look modernistic while stained glass shower doors look artsy, Victorian or period style. Oak seats and tanks including antique and tall ones mounted high on the wall make bathroom look traditional while modern bathroom interiors call for low-profile commodes mounted on the wall.

People with eclectic tastes or frequently changing taste should choose neutral colours and plain styles that can easily be given a different look by switching a few things here and there. Basic porcelain over cast iron bathtub, porcelain toilet and sink and faucets and showerhead in porcelain glass combinations are traditional.

Basic faucets, such as chrome brass combinations, work best with neutral bathroom schemes. White bathrooms can look both traditional and modern depending on other factors and is a safe choice for every kind of decor. Modern faucets such as gooseneck and waterfall faucets ones are trendy.

Bathroom Colours

Popular bathroom colour themes include the colours of wall, tiles, faucets, accessories, towels and napkins and accents such as potted plants. The traditional bathroom colours are neutral that can easily be given different tones according to your taste, just by changing the accent colours, shower curtains, bathroom rugs, towels and accessories. However, fresh linen white seems a good bathroom colour idea to many people, as it makes the bath look fresh, clean and simple and works well almost all the colours and shades.

Crispy white bathrooms with light tranquil blue accents are quite relaxing and have spa-like feel. They can carry clear glass accessories and sterling silver fixtures and hardware finish well.

People who would like elite decor in their baths can choose gold or taupe paint and tile colours with black accents. It can be kept light and airy, if done properly. Bathtub with black exteriors and bisque interiors and edges, polished brass faucets, ginger-glazed medium colour maple wood vanities with black granite and bisque sinks, beige colour floor tiles and shower walls and accent tiles and chair rail tile all in the same colour perfectly compliment the royal colour bathroom theme.

Creamy white bathroom walls and aqua blues and greens as accent colours that remain the popular favourite theme with many people.

White walls and cabinetry, pale aqua floor tiles, accessories in darker aqua shades, towels in complimentary colours and shower curtains having a bit of all the colours as the unifying factor make a beautiful bathroom

If you are living in rented apartments and cannot change the colour of tiles, use accessories to add accent colours, highlight the colours you like and downplay the ones you don't like. Pastels of old times can be revved up with popular chocolate-brown accessories such as towel racks and curtains.

Colour of mirror frames can be one such accent colour.

Do not use dark colours in bathrooms that don't get enough natural light or use ample of artificial light to compensate for it. Dim light in dark bathrooms make them too dark to shave or apply makeup. Too odd a colour in the bath can actually look frightening in the mornings, so steer clear of lime green, peach and certain shades of yellow.

Bath Accessories

Classy and elegant fixtures and bath accessories can turn your bathroom into a personal retreat while adding a creative and fun touch to your bathroom and may increase your comfort level in the bath too.

It is necessary that the bathroom always remains neat and clean and is germ-free. Master bathrooms in modern homes built on larger scale are a popular tend these days and they may be as large and luxurious as the bedrooms in the house, so you should pay special attention to the basic bathroom accessories that define the look of the bathroom, such as bathroom mirrors, towel holders, shower curtains, holders to keep tissue, shampoo and holders, toothbrushes and paste; soap dishes and lotion dispensers.

While pondering on how to choose bathroom and bathtub accessory, make sure that you do not buy too much or too less. You may keep as many bathroom accessories in luxurious bathrooms as you want, as long as you have enough space for them and bathroom does not look too cluttered or crowded.

Do not overdo bathroom accessories or you may have to compromise on the organised look of your bathroom. Bathroom accessories make bathroom environment more appealing and can be bought based on a theme that goes with your bathroom design and style theme. Right accessories can give a unique, creative and different look to our bath space. A simple bathtub accessory such as a rack that fits on one end of the bath can make the soap and bathing lotions easily accessible to while bathing and is a good idea.

Replace bathroom furniture set that sits unutilised in the bathroom with functional bath accessories that hel to relax and add warmth and coziness to the bath. Fresh towels kept neatly on a nearby towel rack ready to use after the shower or hanging on a towel holder in the bathroom wall cabinet are just priceless.

Bathroom accessories also include aroma extracts and essential oils that soothe with their fragrances as you massage them onto your body can occupy a place on your bathroom counters.

You can recreate the spat at home or add romance to the day and pamper yourself by having a bubble bath in the tub strewn with dried or fresh flower petals or coloured soap beads that serve as bathtub accents.

Colour coordinate bathroom accessories and towels and you may even use a family of colours, such as blended reds, oranges or pinks, with green highlights and summer bathrooms bedecked with wethful yellows.

You can find soap dispensers, soap dishes, toothbrush holders and tissue boxes along with other bathroom accessories that can be grouped together as a theme. Find the matching ones and use them to make your bathroom look more attractive.

You can change the look of your bathroom every month or change of season by just changing the bathroom accessory sets and coordinate the colours of bath curtains, towels, hand towels and items around the washbasin items, such as candles and magazine racks to go with them.

Magazine racks are for people who love to read while soaking in the bath. Make sure that the accessories you are using are easy to clean and maintain and can resist moisture and dampness. A shower massager can help ease the tension and relax before going to bed and a fog free shower mirror will help you to shave better.

Expensive designer baths are creatively planned and indulgent and can use crystal bowl washbasins. A stylish, contemporary but small bathroom can use top cabinets; space saving radiators that can be used as towel rails too and may be a built-in seat for a luxurious touch or comfort place for the elderly. A light, simple bathroom carpet in a neutral shade suits contemporary bath decor much more than a heavy and plush rug. Other types of bathroom accessory ideas include pillar taps, bath panels, floor coverings, bathroom cabinets, shelving, window treatments, such as blinds and curtains, towel rails, bins and mirrors.

■ ■ ■

More titles are available in
General Books Series

4263/3, Ansari Road,
Darya Ganj, New Delhi-110002
Ph.: 32903912, 23280047, 9811594448
E-mail: lotus_press@sify.com
www.lotuspress.co.in